D1246954

MY FATHER IL DUCE

MY FATHER IL DUCE

A Memoir by Mussolini's Son

———◆◆———

Romano Mussolini

Introductory Essay by Alexander Stille

Translated from the original Italian by Ana Stojanovic

Kales Press

Kenneth Kales, Publisher
John Sollami, Project Editor
Benedetto Mosca, Personal Assistant and Translator for Romano Mussolini
Marsha Kunin, Proofreader
Jamie Wynne, Editorial Assistant
Jeffrey Sandler, Editorial Consultant

Cover design by Linda McKnight
Ana Stojanovic, Translator from the original Italian
Ms. Stojanovic would like to thank Heather Ciociola and Carmen Ferrigno for their careful and thoughtful reading of the translation, as well as Andrei Campeanu, whose knowledge of military history and armaments proved to be invaluable. Thanks are also due to Dr. Michael Magera and Dr. Miroslav Djokic for their assistance with medical terminology.

Copyright © 2004 RCS Libri S.p.A., Milano, in Italian
Copyright © 2006 Kales Press
Text copyright © 2006 Romano Mussolini
Introductory Essay copyright © Alexander Stille
Photographs © Farabolafoto, RCS Periodici, Getty Images, and Corbis

All rights reserved. First edition

Library of Congress Cataloging-in-Publication Data

Mussolini, Romano.
   [Duce, mio padre. English]
   My father, il Duce : a memoir by Mussolini's son / Romano Mussolini ;
introductory essay by Alexander Stille ; translated from the original
Italian by Ana Stojanovic. — 1st ed.
      p. cm.
   ISBN-13: 978-0-9670076-8-7 (hardcover : alk. paper)
   ISBN-10: 0-9670076-8-2 (hardcover : alk. paper)
   1. Mussolini, Benito, 1883-1945. 2. Mussolini, Benito,
1883-1945—Family. 3.   Mussolini, Romano. 4.   Heads of state—Italy—
Biography. 5.
Italy—Politics and government—1922-1945. I. Title.
   DG575.M8 M8353813
   945.091092—dc22
   [B]

                                        2006023225

Without limiting the rights under copyright reserved above, no part of this publi-cation may be reproduced, stored in or introduced into a retrieval system, or transmitted in any form or by any means (electronic, mechanical, photocopying, recording or otherwise), without the prior written permission of both the copy-right owner and the publisher.

There are three classes of people:
Those who see.
Those who see when they are shown.
Those who do not see.

—Leonardo da Vinci

Contents

Introductory Essay

Alexander Stille

ROMANO MUSSOLINI, THE YOUNGEST CHILD OF BENITO MUSSOLINI, was not what people expected in the offspring of a fascist dictator. A gracious, smiling, and unpretentious man, he made his living for years traveling up and down the Italian peninsula playing jazz piano with his band, *The Romano Mussolini All Stars*. For most of his life he steered clear of politics, even playing under an assumed name during the first years after World War II. He was animated by a genuine love of jazz and toured with some of the greatest figures in 20th-century jazz Chet Baker, Lionel Hampton, and Dizzy Gillespie, among others. His love for jazz itself, dominated by black American musicians, already suggested a streak of independence and even dissent. Its circulation was greatly limited in fascist Italy as his father, Il Duce, tried to root out degenerate foreign influences from the Italian landscape. This position did not apply to the dictator's own family: Romano first encountered jazz when he listened to a vinyl record played by his older brother, Vittorio.

Yet, toward the end of his life, Romano revealed a different side of his character, publishing two books of memoirs that offered a much more sympathetic, positive portrait of Mussolini, not only as a father but as a historical figure. The books are of a piece with their time. Italy's formerly neofascist party, the National Alliance, was brought into the government and the political mainstream by Silvio Berlusconi, the television magnate who became prime minister first in 1994 and again in 2001. The National Alliance's leader, Gianfranco Fini, while pledging loyalty to Italian democracy, referred to Mussolini as "the greatest statesman of the 20th century", a view he later repudiated. One of the new deputies representing the National Alliance in parliament was Alessandra Mussolini, Romano's daughter, who often defends her infamous grandfather and is still active in politics today. And during Berlusconi's second government from 2001 to 2006, a kinder, gentler fascism began to emerge in the public discourse. Berlusconi himself insisted that "fascism never killed anyone, and sent its political opponents on vacation," referring to the regime's practice of placing political dissidents under a kind of house arrest in remote areas far from their native towns. (He said nothing about the approximately 3,000 political opponents who were killed during fascism's rise to power, the much smaller number (approximately 30) who were beaten to death or executed during Mussolini's time in office, and the thousands who were held in prison during the 20-year history of fascism. Of course, we are not mentioning the hundreds of thousands of Italians and non-Italians killed in Mussolini's wars). But by 2005, after *My Father Il Duce* was published and became a best seller in Italy, Romano Mussolini could be seen on television offering a highly sympathetic portrait of his father as largely a caring, sensitive *paterfamilias* rather than one of the inventors of 20th-century totalitarianism. Although he criticized some of his father's decisions, he said in one interview that 90 percent of what his father had done was positive.

Writing the introductory essay to *My Father Il Duce* is a bit like writing the warning label on a powerful drug that has its uses but must be taken with care and knowledge of its possible side effects. The greatest benefit, perhaps, is understanding the evasions and self-deceptions of a certain kind of revisionist history and the conscious and unconscious manipulation of memory involved in learning to accept the unacceptable.

Romano Mussolini, who died on February 3, 2006, was not, to put it mildly, a professional historian, but he was an eyewitness to the family life of Benito Mussolini from his birth in 1928 until Il Duce's death in 1945.

The book's appeal to readers has been to offer a human portrait of a man often portrayed in recent decades purely as a dictator and a monster. While Romano's narration of historical facts, including those of which he was a first- or secondhand witness, is highly suspect and often flat-out wrong, the feelings of filial affection and love are real and entirely comprehensible. Mussolini as family man was hardly conventional. As a young firebrand socialist, Mussolini does not appear to have believed in marriage. He and Romano's mother, Rachele Guidi, had their first child out of wedlock. At the same time, Mussolini conducted many different love affairs and also fathered a child, Benito Albino, whom he recognized as his own by another woman, Ida Dalser. And when Mussolini went off to fight in World War I, he appears to have referred to Dalser as his wife so that she and their child could receive some public assistance. Rachele, in the end, won out, and she and Mussolini were married in a civil ceremony in 1915. Ten years later, they celebrated a religious wedding at a time when Mussolini, now in power, was seeking to ingratiate himself with the Catholic church.

Romano gives us a portrait of a man genuinely attached to his family and, although his infidelities continued, he does appear to have had a powerful bond with his wife, Rachele, a simple country girl from Mussolini's native region of Emilia-

Romagna, on whose unshakable loyalty, toughness, and peasant shrewdness Il Duce appears to have relied. Since Romano's most vivid memories of his father are of his final years, when the boy had reached adolescence and was more aware of what was happening around him, the portrait of Mussolini that emerges here is that of a bumbler whose wife frequently had a surer grip on reality than Italy's totalitarian leader. After Mussolini was voted out of office by the formerly compliant fascist Grand Council in July of 1943, Rachele strongly urged her husband not to go to his appointment with the king the following day to present his resignation. Rachele insisted it was a trap, and, indeed, Mussolini was arrested as he left the meeting something that Il Duce, used to slavish adulation, could not conceive of. The early Mussolini, a brilliant propagandist and tactician, had outflanked many more established political forces in taking over the Italian state through his lack of scruples and his ruthless pursuit of power.

Although he enjoyed absolute power, Mussolini did not use it to amass vast personal wealth. It is no doubt true, as Romano relates, that Rachele made her children finish everything on their dinner plates when they were living rent free in the villa of Prince Torlonia in Rome, as they did when the family lived in various spartan apartments while Mussolini led the life of the penniless socialist revolutionary.

Mussolini, like most Italian husbands, came home for lunch and liked simple meals of soup or pasta. He had little taste for the high life, the social whirl of the Roman aristocracy, or the royal court that formed around the Italian royal family. He tended to spend his evenings at home with his family. Romano tells us that he often relaxed by watching movies after dinner in a little screening room set up in Villa

Torlonia. Curiously, according to his son, Mussolini had a preference for Hollywood comedies, his favorites being films by Charlie Chaplin, Buster Keaton, Laurel and Hardy, and Harold Lloyd, this at a time when Il Duce was trying to stamp out foreign influences from Italian culture, even going so far as to eliminate the handshake as a decadent modern import, to be replaced by reinstituting the ancient Roman salute (a straight arm raised at about a sixty-degree angle). Mussolini's favorite actor, apparently, was Chaplin, and in particular, his films *Modern Times* and *The Gold Rush*. Unfortunately, there is no mention of his seeing Chaplin's *The Great Dictator*, made in 1940, whose unforgettable portrait of Benzini Napaloni, the "Dictator of Bacteria," satirized Mussolini himself and predicted the fall of fascist dictatorships when World War II was just beginning.

Romano describes his father as stern but affectionate:

> *He never raised his voice, but one of his famous stern looks was enough to make us nervous. I must admit, however, that this would seldom occur. In fact, as soon as my father would notice that one of us was blushing or casting an anxious glance at the others, he would change subjects to relieve the tension.*

The tenderness that evidently existed between father and son is illustrated with some poignancy by a few domestic details. Romano, used to spend hours sitting in a wicker armchair listening to music from a phonograph amplified by a large horn. When the family moved to Rome from Romagna, it was Mussolini, Romano writes, who arranged to have the phonograph and his son's favorite armchair brought to their new residence in Rome. Romano relates how he used to spend hours alone in the attic of Villa Torlonia, looking at the sky. One day, he climbed the ladder to the attic to find a telescope his father had procured for him, anticipating a secret wish he had harbored but never articulated. *At times he seemed to live more for others than for himself,* Romano writes.

There is little question that Mussolini was especially fond of his eldest child, Edda, an intelligent, headstrong young woman who married the glamorous young count Galeazzo Ciano, whom Il Duce made his foreign minister. Edda was one of the few people on close enough terms with Italy's dictator to argue and disagree with him. There is also little question that Mussolini was genuinely shaken when his second son, Bruno, was killed in a test flight of a new military aircraft during World War II. Mussolini went on to write a personal memoir about his dead son entitled *Parlo con Bruno* (*Speaking with Bruno*).

The human portrait of Mussolini as a caring husband and father is part of a larger effort to distance him from his closest political ally, Adolf Hitler, with whom he is invariably linked. Indeed, Hitler's own sexual ambiguity and eccentricity are part of his profile as a not quite human fanatic and madman. Hitler never married and never, as far as we know, fathered any children. In his past was the strange episode of the suicide of his niece, Geli Raubal, a twenty-year-old girl who came to live with him in Munich and with whom he appears to have been infatuated. He made her a kind of prisoner in his apartment until she shot and killed herself with Hitler's own gun in 1931. There was also the long but childless relationship with Eva Braun, which finally ended in marriage and their mutual suicide in Hitler's bunker in Berlin just before the war was lost.

Mussolini, before solidifying his "Pact of Steel" with Hitler, went out of his way to distinguish fascism from National Socialism. "Fascism is a regime that is rooted in the great cultural traditions of the Italian people; fascism recognizes the right of the individual, it recognizes religion and family. National Socialism, on the other hand, is savage barbarism." Mussolini's family life, shown frequently in photographs and news reels at the time, was very much a part of the regime's presentation of itself.

But there is also a darker side to Mussolini's family life, which does not reflect well on Mussolini or on the type of regime he created in fascist Italy. Although he acknowledged paternity of his illegitimate son, Benito Albino, the child's mother, Ida Dalser, went on to become something of a nuisance and an embarrassment, bursting into the offices of the newspaper Mussolini was editing and denouncing him for neglecting her and their child. Mussolini tried to have her arrested in order to get her out of the way, something he had no difficulty doing after he came to power in 1922. When she renewed her public criticism of Mussolini for his ill treatment of his illegitimate family, he, in 1925, forcibly confined her to a mental institution where she was kept against her will and the wishes of her family until her death in 1937. Even crueler, the fascist regime strictly forbade the young Benito Albino from ever seeing his mother again and he too, in 1935, was confined to an insane asylum where he died seven years later at the age of only twenty-six. Her letters, many of which survive, testify both to her substantial sanity and to her desperate desire to rejoin her son and family. Particularly tragic are the words she sent to her distant son as she lay on her deathbed. "Benito, don't cry. I will take my heart with me into the grave." Beyond demonstrating the extreme personal cruelty of which Mussolini was capable, the story of Il Duce's illegitimate son also shows the extraordinary limitations to individual freedom and the frequent abuse of power by the totalitarian system of fascism.

The existence of Mussolini's illegitimate son was so well known that Romano Mussolini feels the need to acknowledge it in his memoir. But the skeletal and slanted account of it in *My Father Il Duce* is typical of the half-truths, evasions, and self-deceptions that characterize this memoir:

> *Even at the height of the fascist regime, this woman continued to declare herself Mussolini's real wife, presenting their son Benito Albino as proof.... Through the end of 1922, the year of the March on Rome, her continued appearances were a nightmare for my father. I never spoke to him about it, but I know that he wasn't insensitive to her suffering. Especially since the poor woman, who simply couldn't resign herself to staying away from him, eventually grew extremely depressed and began to behave more irrationally.... She fell gravely ill and began to go in and out of hospitals.*

From this, one would never suppose that Ida Dalser was held against her will, prevented from seeing her own son, and had actually escaped the insane asylum in Venice but was hunted down and brought back there by fascist police. Romano probably never bothered to look into the facts of his poor half-brother's life but it does not prevent him from writing: *I never spoke to [my father] about it, but I know that he wasn't insensitive to her suffering.* The sentence, like many sentences in this book, is worth analyzing for its strategies of deception and self-deception. First, he tells us that he has no direct knowledge of his father's feelings about Ida Dalser, and then he writes with declarative self-assurance that he *knows* that his father cared about her suffering. However, this assertion is qualified by the double negative, *wasn't insensitive to her suffering*, which is a way of saying and unsaying something at the same time, covering the fact that Romano is not, in fact, in a position to say anything at all about Mussolini's feelings about the mother of his child, whom he abandoned and persecuted. Yet this doesn't prevent him from making broad generalizations either about a story he seems to know very little about. The account serves as a model for Romano's narrative. Assumptions are made that are highly favorable to Mussolini. At the same time, Romano shows a shocking lack of curiosity about finding out what really happened to his poor little half-brother, perhaps out of intellectual and moral laziness, perhaps because the facts might force him to reconsider some of his assumptions and regard his father in a harsher light.

While dispatching the tragic story of Ida Dalser and Benito Albino in a page, Romano Mussolini dedicates a good deal more space to the two other big domestic dramas of the Mussolini family: the execution by firing squad for treason of Mussolini's son-in-law, Galeazzo Ciano, the husband of Il Duce's favorite daughter, Edda; and Mussolini's passionate affair with Claretta Petacci, who was captured and killed together with Il Duce in the last days of the war, and whose body was strung up on a lamppost next to his in Piazzale Loreto in Milan.

Both are, indeed, dramatic stories, even if they have been told often before. Galeazzo Ciano was a rich, upper-class Italian playboy whose courtship of Il Duce's daughter was the ultimate tabloid romance of its day. Their marriage was characterized by persistent rumors of infidelity on both sides and each spouse leading a fairly independent life. Nonetheless, Il Duce's son-in-law was the rising star and presumptive heir apparent of fascism during the late 1930s. Mussolini made Ciano his head of propaganda and then his foreign minister precisely as fascism took its fatal steps of establishing its military alliance with Hitler's Germany. However, after World War II had dragged on for a few years, Ciano became increasingly critical of the Germans and disillusioned with Mussolini's own leadership. His diary, which stretches from 1937 to 1943, is one of the richest records we have of day-to-day life within the fascist regime. In July of 1943, after Anglo-American troops had taken Sicily with surprising ease and were ready to make their way up the Italian boot, the majority of fascist leaders had concluded that the war was lost and that Mussolini had become hopelessly out of touch with reality. They called a meeting of the Fascist Grand Council, which was supposed to be a kind of governing council of fascism but had not met in years, and voted Mussolini out of power after a heated debate lasting into the night. The following day, after Mussolini presented his resignation to King Victor Emmanuel, he was arrested.

In the midst of Italy's hasty and incompetent efforts to extract itself from the war, the Nazis managed to pull off a daring rescue mission that plucked Mussolini from a remote mountaintop resort hotel where he was being held prisoner. Hitler then invaded Italy and installed Mussolini as the head of a new fascist government, the so called Republic of Salò, so called because it had its headquarters in northern Italy near the town of Salò. The new government immediately arrested all those on the Fascist Grand Council they could get their hands on who had voted Mussolini out of office, placed them on trial, and executed them. Edda Mussolini sprang into action and did everything possible to try to save the father of her children. In particular, she tried to offer the Nazis Ciano's secret diaries (whose publication would be highly embarrassing) in exchange for his life. She lobbied her father, who refused to act to save his son-in-law. After her husband's execution, Edda fled the country and vowed never to see her father again. Romano's rendition more or less follows the standard account but with a few significant omissions and additions. He leaves out the fact that Edda and Galeazzo Ciano had been enthusiastic supporters of the alliance with Hitler. He portrays Mussolini as entirely powerless to save his son-in-law, since the Germans would never have considered the possibility of clemency for the coup plotters. Mussolini and his daughter are thus both portrayed as tragic victims: Edda battles nobly to save her husband on behalf of her children, while Mussolini, forced to consider the fate of the nation itself, must accept the inevitability of Ciano's execution.

The story of Mussolini and the unfortunate Claretta Petacci is the stuff of pure pulp romance. Claretta was one of the countless Italian women who fell madly in love with her country's virile leader and was only too happy to accept when called by Mussolini to visit him in his office at Palazzo Venezia. And, with the enthusiastic cooperation of her family, she set herself up in her own apartment as Il Duce's official mistress. A substantial subliterature exists about this love story, books such as *Chi Ama e' Perduto (Who Loves Is Lost)*, which portrays Claretta's passionate love and devotion as blinding her to the risks to her own life. She then courageously accepts almost certain death by remaining at Benito's side until the bitter end. Romano follows this same tradition, adding the melodrama of Rachele's experience of the affair with Claretta. Rachele, according to Romano, was unfazed by Mussolini's other infidelities because she always knew that Il Duce was really hers. But in the case of Claretta, she sensed that Benito had genuinely lost his head for the ravishing young Roman girl. There is a final showdown between the two in which Rachele confronts Claretta at her villa near Salò and then, in an attempt to commit suicide, drinks from a bottle of bleach. Rachele recovers, leading to a tearful reconciliation between her and Mussolini. In order to elevate Mussolini above the level of inconsiderate philanderer, Romano then turns Claretta into a truly heroic figure for whom love was stronger than death and who even courageously fought her captors as she was about to be killed.

While Romano's sometimes bathetic portrayal of this family melodrama is humanly comprehensible, it is also important to see it in context. The emphasis on the purely personal Mussolini has the effect of blurring beyond recognition or eliminating entirely the historical backdrop against which these events occurred. Moreover, the simple fact that Romano Mussolini was only twelve when Italy entered World War II and only began to have a greater comprehension of things at the very end of his father's life, gives us a highly distorted image of Mussolini as an almost pathetic old man buffeted about by events rather than as a protagonist of history with grave responsibilities for Italy's fate between 1922 and 1945. At a certain point, Romano writes of his parents: *They found themselves together in the middle of a war which no one wanted, and whose catastrophic developments no one expected.* Notice the strange passive verb used and the total lack of agency in the sentence: *They found themselves,* as if World War II was something in which Mussolini had no role, indeed, something that *no one wanted.*

In fact, if you read *My Father Il Duce* carefully as well as Romano Mussolini's other book, *Ultimo Atto (The Final Act)*, which deals with some of the same material, you will note that both are laced with a series of absurdly revisionist accounts of historical events and crazy conspiracy theories aimed principally at absolving Mussolini or at least greatly mitigating his heavy responsibility for starting, fomenting, and supporting a series of wars that accounted for more than 55 million dead in the period between 1935 and 1945.

It could not be further from the truth that Mussolini sought to avoid war. War was always seen as the inevitable, natural, and desirable aim of fascism. As Mussolini (with his coauthor, the philosopher Giovanni Gentile) wrote in his definition of fascism in the *Enciclopedia Italiana*, "War alone brings to its highest tension all human energy and puts the stamp of nobility upon the peoples who have courage to meet it. All other trials are substitutes, which never really put men into the position where they have to make the great decision, the alternative of life or death." At another point, Mussolini said, "War is to men what maternity is to women."

Empire and conquest were seen as the natural destiny of a great nation, which Mussolini was determined Italy should become again. Thus, entirely on his own initiative, he invaded Ethiopia, and, in contravention of treaties Italy had signed to not use chemical weapons, he employed mustard gas in conquering and pacifying the much poorer country. As many as 275,000 Ethiopians may have died in the invasion and "pacification" campaign that followed. About 3,000 civilians were massacred in a single weekend after Ethiopian resisters tried to assassinate an Italian general.

In addition, more than 100,000 Libyans died in concentration camps set up by the Italians as part of fascism's efforts to tighten its grip on its colony in North Africa.

Mussolini firmly believed that it was only through war that Italy, which had become soft and pleasure-loving, would regain the natural greatness it had lost when the Roman Empire fell and Italy was thereafter subjected to foreign invasions and domination. Mussolini enthusiastically sent troops to the Spanish Civil War in part as a means of reshaping the national character. The war in Spain, Il Duce said, would give the Italian middle class "a sound kick in the shins.... and when that's done, I'll invent something else so that the character of the Italians forms itself through war."

In 1937 Mussolini entered into the so called "Pact of Steel" with Nazi Germany, a military alliance that bound the two countries to fight at each other's side in the event of war. Hitler discussed with Mussolini his imminent plans for taking over the rest of Europe, although Mussolini explained that Italy would need several years to get its army into top shape. Mussolini joined the Axis precisely because he believed that Germany was destined to rule Europe and he wanted to be on the winning side.

In 1938, with no pressure from the Germans, Mussolini adopted anti-Jewish racial laws, which reduced Italy's Jews to the rank of second-class citizens and ultimately made it possible for the Germans to identify and deport them.

At times, Mussolini's war-making was accomplished for the pettiest motives of personal vanity. He invaded Albania in 1939 partly as a reaction to the German occupation of Czechoslovakia. Hitler had not informed his Italian ally of his imminent move and Mussolini wanted to show that two could play that game. Too bad for the Albanians.

Hitler, as it turned out, did not wait for Italy to be ready to start World War II, which officially began with the invasion of Poland in the summer of 1939. Italy remained on the sideline for nearly a year and might have sat out the war entirely, as Spanish dictator Francisco Franco did. Mussolini remained undecided, caught between his generals' advice that the army was not ready for a major war and his desire for conquest and glory. In June of 1940, with the French army close to collapse and German troops nearing Paris, Mussolini decided also to invade France. His greatest fear was that the war would end before he could earn a place at the victors' table.

In 1941, although the Axis powers had their hands full fighting most of Europe, Mussolini, following his own military instincts, invaded Greece. Italian troops were pushed back into Albania, which forced Hitler to send troops to bail the Italians out. The cost of this demonstration of national greatness: 15,000 Greeks killed, 28,000 Italians dead or missing, and an indirect consequence, more than 60,000 Greek Jews deported and killed by the Nazis.

When Hitler invaded Russia in June of 1941, Mussolini insisted on sending some 200,000 Italian troops too, even though Hitler specifically didn't want them, and they were completely unequipped for a Russian winter. Mussolini actually complained that not enough Italian soldiers were dying, as would befit a great nation at war. Tens of thousands of Italians died in the campaign and tens of thousands more were taken prisoner by the Germans and died in Nazi concentration camps when Italy tried to withdraw from the war in 1943.

The final results of Mussolini's recklessness, vanity, and poor judgment: 306,000 Italian soldiers killed; 145,000 Italian civilians dead; 8,000 Italian Jews deported and killed, for a grand total of 459,000 deaths. This total does not include, of course, the hundreds of thousands killed by Italians. As a military commander, Mussolini inevitably gets a badly failing grade. He consistently trusted his own "infallible" intuition over professional military advice, making one disastrous move after another.

Almost nothing of this appalling record appears in either of Romano Mussolini's books, *My Father Il Duce* and *The Final Act*. Because the disaster of Italy's role in World War II will not disappear, the aim of Romano Mussolini and the cruder revisionists is to try to assign blame for it elsewhere or to lessen Mussolini's responsibility.

For example, Romano Mussolini claims that he hastily destroyed a series of documents left behind by his father that would have changed the way the history of World War II is viewed:

> *What did those pieces of paper contain? Undoubtedly, there were several documents of historical significance. I remember some pertaining to the trial of Verona and others to my father's relations with Germany, France, and England, dated before the war broke out. They contained proof of Il Duce's efforts to prevent the conflict, an important subject whose relevance historians have only recently come to recognize.*

Indeed, it is a standard theme of Italian revisionism, to which Romano gives credence, that Mussolini carried with him at the time of his capture and death a suitcase full of top-secret documents that he felt would protect him if he made it safely across the Swiss border. Much is made of a supposed secret correspondence between Mussolini and Churchill that would have been fatally embarrassing to Churchill had it ever come to light. Indeed, revisionists like to point out that in the late 1940s, Churchill took a trip to the lake country of Northern Italy, supposedly to indulge in his passion as an amateur painter. The real purpose of the trip, they say, was to recover these embarrassing documents. Does anyone really believe that if there were documents of such importance floating around that Churchill, by then an old man, would have collected them himself rather than sending agents of His Majesty's Secret Service? Besides, what could this secret correspondence have possibly revealed? That Churchill was courting and flattering Mussolini in hopes of keeping him from entering the war or perhaps that he was trying to get Mussolini to make a separate peace with the Allies rather than press on fighting at Hitler's side? Or that Mussolini was looking for a way out of the war, as Romano maintains? This would hardly be surprising. It was very much both British and American policy to try to court Mussolini in order to keep him from joining Hitler's war efforts, and they were happy to make a separate peace with Italy when it was ready to abandon the war. None of this changes Mussolini's responsibility. What we know for sure is that he chose Hitler over Churchill, that he chose to enter the war, and that he chose, against the rising tide of dissent within his own regime, to continue fighting when others had already concluded that the war was lost.

Readers will note that Romano Mussolini goes to great lengths to show that the British were determined that Mussolini should be killed immediately upon capture rather than consigned to a war-crimes tribunal. The clear implication is that by killing him they would be rid of a dangerous witness.

At another point, Romano Mussolini writes:

> *Few are aware, however, I can confirm this with cer-*
> *tainty having consulted previously undisclosed documents,*
> *that my father's arrest on July 25th by the king prevented Il*
> *Duce from executing a sensational political maneuver that he*
> *had studied on several occasions with his closest collaborators.*
>
> *What was the maneuver in question? "In the midst of*
> *this darkness," my father would say, "I don't rule out the*
> *possibility of a final day of sunshine." Puzzling words, ones*
> *he also addressed to his son-in-law Galeazzo Ciano on more*
> *than one occasion. In essence, Il Duce hoped to somehow*
> *extricate Italy from the war. This, in part, explains his*
> *strangely passive reaction when faced with the Grand*
> *Council's vote of no-confidence. He wanted to put his cards*
> *on the table with the Germans and to agree on an inde-*
> *pendent plan of action for the common good. This before the*
> *situation grew worse with the involvement of the United*
> *States, a development whose devastating consequences he in*
> *fact intuited long before Hitler.*

The truth of the matter is that Mussolini was deposed by his "closest collaborators" precisely because he stubbornly insisted on continuing the war, against the advice of an increasing majority within the regime who had decided the war was lost. Moreover, in typical fashion, Romano says he has consulted *previously undisclosed documents,* but then doesn't cite a single document in support of his statement.

Additionally, this account is flatly contradicted by other things that Romano writes, namely, that Mussolini continued to believe the war could be won:

It's true. My sister and I wouldn't give up hope. The trust we had in our father's resourcefulness was stronger than anything else. On July 20 [1943] Il Duce met Hitler in Germany and, upon his return, told us about the secret factories producing "Flying Bombs," the famous V1 and V2 that everyone was talking about for years. He himself had seen the deadly arsenals and had no doubts that once they were put in use, the enemy would have no recourse.

The V1 and V2 bombs were Anna Maria's and my favorite subject. In her wisdom, our mother shuddered. Il Duce, though, truly believed in our German ally's capacity to recover, or at least he forced himself to believe so.

So, at one point, Romano tells us that Mussolini had a brilliant plan for pulling out of the war, and at the same time, he tells us that Mussolini was convinced that the war could still be won.

Indeed, in *The Final Act*, Romano goes even further, making the preposterous claim that the Germans had developed the atomic bomb before the Allies and that the bombs the Americans exploded in Hiroshima and Nagasaki were, in all likelihood, German: "Only recently have we learned that, thanks to those scientists, Hitler had a nuclear reactor for enriching uranium. But there's more. I have always heard that after the war, the Americans found atomic arms in Germany. It's not improbable that this accelerated the perfection of the bomb dropped on Hiroshima." The evidence that Romano cites is from his brother, Vittorio Mussolini, whose only proof is that the Hiroshima bomb was dropped three months after the defeat of Germany. Romano writes, "How can one not be struck by the lapse in time between these two dates?" *The Final Act*, p. 110.

This, of course, is contradicted by all available documentation. We know a great deal about the German weapons program, and one of its most striking features was how far behind it was in atomic research. Indeed, the Nazi's chief scientist, Werner Heisenberg, used this fact as part of his defense against the charges of war crimes, insisting that he had deliberately slowed down the development of a German bomb. Moreover, the claim is patently absurd on the face of it: does anyone believe that if Hitler had had a weapon that would have changed the direction of the war in his favor he wouldn't have used it?

But the claim of the German secret weapons program makes Mussolini's faith in Germany's ability to win the war more plausible, even though it contradicts Romano's own claim that Mussolini was really suing for peace and searching for a way out of the war. In short, Romano Mussolini's account of the end of the war is a mass of contradictions and absurdities.

This, in turn, is contradicted by yet a third account (in *The Final Act*) from the same year, 1943, in which Romano portrays Mussolini as disconsolate and without hope. "The psychological collapse of my father was already evident in 1943. I say this because it was around halfway through that year that I made the following notes: 'I see Il Duce as increasingly less interested in the events going on around him. There are days when he is totally absent. His thoughts are elsewhere and he responds mechanically to the questions he is asked. Even we in the family feel him to be increasingly farther away and detached.'"

This account, supposedly from notes taken at the time and therefore less subject to a nostalgic rewriting of history, corresponds more to the accounts of a Mussolini who has lost his grip on Italy's deteriorating situation, prompting his ouster on July 25, 1943.

Finally, in *The Final Act*, Romano quotes his father giving an explanation for his own behavior in taking Italy to war and keeping it at war that comes surprisingly close to the known record: "Oceanic crowds, grandiose parades, that atmosphere of epic vitality and of military glory that one breathed in the Germany of Hitler: all this blinded me, I must admit it. I, too, loved the mystic and heroic life. I thought my future lay with the alliance with Germany. I wanted to transform Italy, a nation of artists, into a people of warriors.... The lives of millions of people depended on me, and in the light of what happened, this thought gives me no peace." *The Final Act*, p. 37.

What Romano Mussolini never comes to terms with is the very system of fascism his father set up, the 90 percent of fascism that he judges as having been positive. The suspension of civil and political liberties, the absolute rule of the fascist party, and the cult of personality around Mussolini with its absurd slogans such as "Mussolini is always right" contributed overwhelmingly to the disasters of the war. The system had no accountability; mistakes and atrocities could be swept under the rug. Mussolini was free to ignore public sentiment, professional advice, and dissenting opinion in his own party and did so in plunging Italy into World War II. In the absence of anything to check him, Mussolini's regime became a kind of echo chamber in which he himself appears to have come to believe his own propaganda, that Italy's "eight million bayonets" were an invincible force, that the British were a decadent people with no aptitude for war, that the United States, despite having become the premier industrial power in the world, was a paper tiger. And so his own shallow, ill-informed opinions became unchallenged dogmas that contributed in no small measure to the undoing of Italy and the deaths of hundreds of thousands.

MY FATHER IL DUCE

Preface

The last time I saw my father, Il Duce, was the morning of April 17, 1945, on Lago di Garda, in Gargnano, seat of the Republic of Salò. Only eleven days remained until the moment of his death, when he was killed with Claretta Petacci, their bodies hoisted on display in the chaos of Piazzale Loreto.

At Villa Feltrinelli, where I was staying with my mother, my sister Anna Maria, and my brother Bruno's widow Gina, I was playing the piano in a room with a view of the interior courtyard reserved for automobiles. I was sounding out the notes of Franz Lehar's *Merry Widow*. My father had received the Hungarian composer's original score as a gift, and he was delighted every time I played his music. So, when I saw him enter the room that morning I thought he wanted to hear me play for a few moments, standing behind me, as was his custom on other occasions.

Instead, he embraced me. "Ciao, Romano," he said in a low and melancholy voice not his own. "Continue playing."

He exited into the courtyard and got in the car that was waiting to take him to Milan where, he assured my mother, he would remain for two or three days at the most," the time he needed to determine whether resistance to the Allies' advance was still possible. He wore his military uniform. I turned to the window and saw him look back for a final farewell, waving his right hand as the car started.

Romano Mussolini
Rome, Italy
January 2006

CHAPTER I

Franco Could Have Saved Him

My father was born on July 29, 1883; I came into the world—the fourth of his five children with Rachele Guidi—on September 26, 1927. At the time of our last meeting, therefore, he was 61 years and 9 months old; I was 17 years and 7 months old. I had had all the time I needed to get to know him and bear witness to, if not play a role in, many events that are debated to this day.

In writing this book, I wanted not only to share my memories as his son, but also, by contributing new elements of the story, to help shed light on certain aspects of Il Duce's life.

Some will wonder whether, after so many years, anything remains to be revealed and whether any unpublished details are worthy of consideration. My answer is, "Yes." Much history still needs to be written because reconstructions are often tainted by emotion. Above all, I maintain that one of the fundamental chapters of my father's life, the one relating to *why* he died in the manner in which everyone is familiar, is yet to be completely understood.

Is it true, for example, that on the night of July 24, 1943, when he realized that Dino Grandi and the other members of the Fascist Grand Council were preparing to depose him, my father could have blocked them inside the Palazzo Venezia and perhaps even had them killed?

Is it true that when the Allies were moving up the peninsula after landing in Sicily, he refused to react because he had a revolutionary plan in mind and intended to launch negotiations for a separate peace?

Is it true that Hitler, whom my father met at Feltre on July 19, 1943, six days prior to the king arresting my father and subsequently confining him at Gran Sasso, wanted to have a detachment of the SS protect him—a development that would have changed the course of events?

Finally, is it true that when Galeazzo Ciano, my sister Edda's husband, was tried and sentenced to death in Verona during the time of the Republic of Salò, my father tried to pass a provision to freeze all legal proceedings until the end of the war?

I can attest that, through to the very end, my father could have been saved. In fact, there was a plan—arranged to the finest of details—for getting him to safety. And if he didn't seek shelter, it was only by choice. "I don't want to beg for salvation," he would say, "while the finest of men are sacrificing themselves for me and for Italy's dignity." The escape plan was conceived by Luigi Gatti—my father's personal secretary, later executed at Dongo—and by my brother Vittorio. Gatti was married to a Spanish noblewoman with whom he had a son, Alfredo, who is to this day like a brother to me. Even he remembers, as do I, how events were supposed to unfold. On the waters of the lake in front of Villa

Feltrinelli, a hydroplane was to have descended at dusk, piloted by one of my father's loyal supporters. My brother and Luigi Gatti, having sedated Il Duce, were to take him to the embankment and from there lift him on board. The hydroplane was to head for the coast of Spain where some of Mrs. Gatti's workers—she owned a large farm in the center of the country—were to arrive in two cars and take him into their care.

Everything had been arranged to ensure that every trace of Il Duce would be lost. But there's more. In Spain, my father was to have enjoyed Franco's protection, and Franco was to have then found a way to save him by reaching an agreement with the Americans.

I say this because in 1963, in Madrid, I met the then 71-year-old Francisco Franco, who had never forgotten his rise to power in 1939 thanks to my father's and Hitler's support. Extremely thin, only his eyes active and alert, the great general looked like a centenarian. He was pessimistic. "The communists will win," he told me, "because there are millions and millions of poor in the world, and the poor will always be communists." He revealed his intentions to restore the monarchy, which he in fact did six years later, and to name as his successor the young Juan Carlos, passing over Juan Carlos's father. "It will be a painful transition," he added, sensing my misgivings. "All the decisions I've made in my life were sooner or later accepted." In his time, Franco expected my father to seek refuge in Spain.

———

IL DUCE, IT IS TRUE, wanted to meet his destiny, a destiny that, in part—and I will attempt to explain why—he himself rendered inescapable.

I was extremely attached to my father. In his last days, after we moved to Lago di Garda, I was very close to him, more so than in Rome. It is true that, unlike my sister Anna Maria, I lacked the courage to visit him every day at Villa Orsoline where he had established his headquarters while we were living in Villa Feltrinelli. Still, after lunch we would take long walks together, and a beautiful rapport developed between us. As time passes, even the most important and busiest of men become closer to their children. I wasn't fortunate enough to see my father grow old, to feel us become more like brothers, but the sad period during the Republic of Salò certainly fostered our closeness.

Everything was falling apart, and yet, even in February of 1945, Il Duce refused to give up hope. There are those who still do not believe that even to the last he was kept in the dark about negotiations for Italy's surrender under way between the Germans and the Allies. But it is true, and I even heard him tell my mother, "In Germany, Hitler himself took me to the factories manufacturing the arms that will turn the war around. What's important is not to lose faith. The rest will come on its own."

Did he truly believe his own words? The answer to this question is twofold and holds the key to understanding the man. On the one hand, Il Duce knew that the war was lost. The major cities of northern Italy were lying in ruins, and 70 percent of the houses in Milan were destroyed or uninhabitable. The Italian military apparatus had fallen to pieces, and on April 10, 1945, Anglo-American troops launched the final offensive on German positions by reaching the Po River in northern Italy. And General Wolff, the official representative of the German armed forces in Italy, had been summoned by Hitler to return to Berlin. "As well as being a first-rate politician," my mother said to me one day, "Il Duce was an intelligent man and it would be doing him a disservice to think that he didn't understand the situation with all of its desperation."

ON THE OTHER HAND, he was also an incurable dreamer. It's no surprise then that D'Annunzio was the man he most admired. My father had a dream, an illusion he was the first to doubt, but which he nonetheless obstinately cultivated. He planned to reach Valtellina with a group of his most loyal followers. He was assured there would be at least 30,000 troops with whom he could lead the final resistance against the Allies' invasion. For him, this last battle would have represented a sort of purifying sacrifice. "This will be the Thermopylae of Fascism," he used to say. "Like Leonidas and his heroes, I will sacrifice myself to block the enemy's way."

But how were they to reach Valtellina without being intercepted? It was my brother Vittorio, on Il Duce's behalf, who confided a plan of action to the cardinal of Milan, Ildefonso Schuster. The cardinal had been communicating with the Allies for some time in an attempt to render their entrance into the city less bloody. I heard my father tell my mother, "Schuster is a great mediator. I trust him."

She had much less faith in Schuster, but she was wrong. After speaking to Vittorio, Schuster contacted the Allied command via the Nunciature in Switzerland. The response, however, was negative. The Allies demanded the complete and unconditional surrender of the Fascists and were not prepared to offer safe passage for any of them, especially not to Valtellina, which would have resulted in new clashes and, in short, a prolonging of the war.

My father was disappointed with the cardinal's message. In his mind, most likely, he was reliving the nightmare that had been tormenting him for months—his capture and trial staged by the Americans. In one of the last times we dined with him at Villa Feltrinelli, as he rose from the table he said, "I can already see the trial they will stage for me at Madison Square Garden, with the people in the stands looking at me as if I were a caged beast." I also remember him adding, "No, it is better to die with weapons raised. Only this can be an end worthy of my existence."

THE EPILOGUE OF MY FATHER'S LIFE, viewed now from a distance of more than half a century is like an episode from one of the novels he wrote as a young man.

Even more far-fetched was his mistress Claretta Petacci's plan to save him. My mother learned of it only after the war was over. My brother Vittorio and I, however, had been immediately aware of it. It was an absurd plan, clearly lacking any possibility of success, but at the time we grasped for anything.

Claretta had left Villa Fiordaliso (the "house of the dead," as my mother used to call it, having never seen anyone enter or leave there) and joined my father in Milan. She was accompanied, as usual, by her brother Marcello—a man the entire organization despised because of the privileged status he enjoyed thanks to his sister, and because he infamously lacked scruples. But when it came to protecting Claretta, he became a different person. He tried to help his sister in every way, which is what he did when she asked him to devise a plan for bringing both her and Il Duce together to safety.

Marcello was to procure an automobile similar to those in which my father traveled, a black Alfa Romeo, and he was to have it driven into a wall to simulate an accident. The wreckage would then be burned, and from it the emergency workers would extract the disfigured cadaver of a man in a military uniform. This act would, in short, be a murder, but the sacrifice of the poor man killed in place of Il Duce would supposedly lead everyone to believe that my father had died in an attempt to flee. Then he and Claretta were to seek safety in Switzerland under assumed names, and from there, the couple was to continue on to Australia via a series of transfers in rented airplanes.

CHAPTER 2

Behind the Scenes of the Arrest at Villa Savoia

On July 25, 1943, my father rose, as usual, at eight o'clock, having rested for a couple of hours after coming home to Villa Torlonia at four o'clock in the morning. He had just attended the dramatic meeting of the Grand Council in which nineteen of the twenty-eight voters, including his son-in-law Galeazzo Ciano, had betrayed him.

That early morning he came home gloomy and despondent, and my mother, referring to the conspirators who had signed Dino Grandi's order of the day, said to him, "I hope you had them all arrested." He responded, "Not yet. I'll do it tomorrow morning." To which she burst out, "Don't you understand that tomorrow morning will be too late! Grandi and his companions, including Galeazzo, will already have disappeared."

Il Duce interrupted this berating by pointing to the telephone and telling my mother to call the general staff in order to find out whether there had been any bombing raids in recent hours. My mother dialed the number and handed him the receiver.

When we saw each other again a few months later, he recounted, "The general staff tried to reassure me by claiming there had been nothing significant to report. In reality, they were lying because only a few hours earlier Bologna had been bombed. All of Italy was in a state of alarm, but I was being kept in the dark. An incredible conspiracy was taking shape around me, or maybe they were colluding with those who wanted catastrophe and defeat."

After the telephone call, my father retired to his room and, without speaking any further, threw himself on the bed, exhausted. It was six o'clock in the morning, and two hours later, he would rise as usual to go to Palazzo Venezia. At nine o'clock, he was already in his office where he received the Japanese ambassador, Shinrokuro Hidaka. He urged the ambassador to apply pressure on his government to induce Hitler to conclude a separate peace with the Soviet Union.

The Soviets had already launched an attack on the eastern front. My father told me, "If Russia had accepted the truce, it would have taken a terrible weight off Germany's shoulders and they could have helped us drive back the enemy we were facing at home. It was only a hope, I confess, because I was perfectly aware that events had already taken an irreversible turn."

I nevertheless had the impression, not only on this occasion but on others as well, that my father did not fully comprehend the implications of the Grand Council's vote of no-confidence. And, above all, he was unaware of one very important fact. The king, upon learning the results of the no-confidence vote, appointed

General Pietro Badoglio as the new head of government. In short, my father was unaware and couldn't even conceive that while he was speaking to the Japanese ambassador, Italy had replaced him.

My mother later explained, "Badoglio was already toasting with his family victory over your father. Meanwhile, your father didn't have the slightest suspicion. He made no attempt to react. He didn't understand that they had decided to oust him." And it was so. In effect, my father still allowed Grandi to present his order of the day, knowing full well that it would mean his ruin. Despite the fact that Il Duce had the militia on his side, as Galbiati and the other loyal Fascist leaders had repeatedly assured him, he didn't try to react. It would have been very easy for him to block Grandi's initiative on the no-confidence vote. He could have done so right up to the last moment of that interminable meeting, by having the militia enter the room after deactivating the door-blocking device. The door control was in front of him—a small push-button apparatus attached to the underside of the long U-shaped table around which the voters were seated.

All Il Duce had to do was to press a button to put an end to the conspirators, and many others in the room would have certainly denounced them as well. Can you imagine a Hitler or a Stalin or any other dictator saying, "All right, you have revoked your confidence and I will step aside"? Since the dawn of time, blood has been spilled in such instances. Stalin, in particular, would have made hundreds of potential adversaries disappear for much less, even before they declared themselves against him.

My father, however, was fascinated with the inescapable. Perhaps he intended, as he indicated to my mother, to have Grandi arrested. But I believe that he expected to regain his position by confronting him face-to-face and reinstating all of his privileges. I say this because I know that my father called Grandi that night before going to bed, but was unable to reach him. I know too that he was deluding himself because he subsequently told us that early that morning, Grand Council officer Scorza telephoned to tell him that Cianetti, and many of the others, wanted to retract their vote of no-confidence brought by Grandi.

At Palazzo Venezia, after the meeting with the Japanese ambassador, Il Duce received a telephone call from Villa Camilluccia where Claretta Petacci had been staying. He had already spoken to her around three that morning before coming home to Villa Torlonia.

Claretta, therefore, already knew the results of the Grand Council's vote. And she also knew that Il Duce had asked his secretary to arrange a meeting with the king, possibly at five o'clock later that day. She was extremely worried and advised him not to go to either Quirinale or to Villa Savoia, the two places where the king would be able to receive him. She also warned him about the newly appointed head of government, General Badoglio. But at that point my father broke out in a sarcastic smile and said, "Badoglio has other things to do. At this hour he's probably playing bocce."

Later that day, at almost three o'clock in the afternoon, Il Duce arrived home at Villa Torlonia and sat down at the table with my mother. "I'm late," my mother told me he said, "because I extended the meeting with General Galbiati (the militia chief) to survey the San Lorenzo neighborhood bombed by the Anglo-American troops last week."

My sister Anna Maria and I were in Riccione with Gina, and Il Duce and my mother were alone. He was pale and pensive. As always, he ate quickly—a hearty soup followed by a plate of boiled vegetables. And, as usual, he drank only water.

My mother and I have reconstructed the events leading up to his arrest later that day at Villa Savoia, which, in effect, signaled the end of Fascism. Il Duce first asked her for news of Anna Maria and me, and then he said, "Today at five o'clock I have to see the king." My mother echoed Claretta's plea. "Don't go to him and do not trust Badoglio." He responded, "I have to see the king because he and I signed the pact with Germany, and we must abide by it. Whether he relieves me of duty or not is secondary. The king first needs to know who the traitors are and authorize me to arrest them."

At that point, the telephone rang three times. It was a call from Villa Savoia. The king would be expecting Il Cavalier Mussolini at five o'clock that afternoon. And the official on the phone specified that he was invited to appear in civilian clothing, not in military uniform.

Comparing my mother's notes with my own, I have been able to reconstruct what happened at that point, including a portion of my parents' impassioned conversation:

"Rachele, which suit should I wear?"

15

"None. You shouldn't go to the king. If he told you to wear civilian clothes, don't you understand that it's in order to arrest you without drawing attention? Listen to me. Last night I told you that this meeting of the Grand Council would be dangerous for you, and you didn't listen. I also told you to have everyone arrested before it began, do you remember?"

While putting on the blue linen suit she had brought for him without his thinking about how hot it would be to wear, my father repeated, "But don't you understand that it's impossible for the king to turn against me? To do so would mean suicide for him."

"And he is your friend?" my mother asked contentiously. "This can't be what you're trying to tell me. Not one of the Savoias is your friend, not even the crown prince who you always protected and downright pulled out of a scandal fifteen years ago. He is just like his father, and he's not important anyway."

At 4:30 P.M., my father's secretary, De Cesare, appeared at Villa Torlonia. It was time to go. De Cesare was holding an envelope that he handed to my mother saying, "In here is Cianetti's retraction of his vote of no-confidence in Il Duce. It reaffirms his opposition to the Grand Council's vote. Please, Signora, take great care of this envelope." It was this very letter that, several months later, saved Cianetti from execution at the trial of Verona.

With the doors already open, my father got into the car that had been waiting for him and De Cesare at the Villa Torlonia entrance. At the very same time, Quinto Navarra, first in charge of Il Duce's office at Palazzo

Venezia, was summoned by Claretta Petacci to the Cybo apartment that had been reserved for her by my father. She was extremely agitated and asked Navarra why Il Duce had not yet arrived at his office. But he couldn't answer her for at least an hour because it was almost five o'clock before he learned that Il Duce had instead been called to see the king. At this point, Claretta took her purse and headed for the exit with Navarra. "I told him not to go to Villa Savoia!"

My father revealed to my mother, "To the last, Galbiati offered to have the militia intervene on my behalf. I reiterated my 'no,' not realizing that at that exact moment, General Castellano, on orders from Badoglio, had already sent a division of grenadiers to Rome to respond to any possible resistance."

Everything was ready at Villa Savoia when my father, at exactly five o'clock as scheduled, passed through the gates of the royal residence on Via Salaria. Il Duce was in a car driven by his faithful Ercole Boratto. He noticed several carabinieri in the gardens, but this didn't strike him as unusual. The king was on the doorstep to the villa and Il Duce approached to greet him. He shook my father's hand and, leading him inside, asked him to report on the previous night's events in detail. Il Duce began to give an account, tending to underplay the events. But the king immediately objected that the Grand Council was an organ of the state and that its decisions were to be respected.

Here's how my father described what happened: "The king was in a state of unusual anxiety. He said to me with clipped speech, 'Things can't go on like this.

Italy is falling to pieces and the soldiers don't want to fight anymore. The mountain regiments sing a song about no longer wanting to fight the war for Mussolini, the most hated man in Italy.'

"I gave no response, devastated by what I was hearing. The king continued, 'You have no more friends and I am the only one you can still count on. But don't worry, nothing will happen to you. I will make sure you are protected. From now on, Field Marshal Badoglio is in charge and I will entrust him with forming a new government to continue the war.'

"I told the king that this was a decision of extreme gravity. I also said that I understood the people's disdain because it is impossible to govern over a long period of time and demand so many sacrifices without provoking resentment. In any case, I wished good luck to any man who would willingly take the situation into his own hands."

It was exactly 5:20 P.M. when the king accompanied Il Duce back to the doorstep. "The king was livid," my father told my brother Vittorio and me. "And he seemed even smaller, almost as if he had shrunk. He shook my hand without looking me in the eyes and went inside again. As I descended the short stairway, I looked for the car in which I had arrived but didn't see it. A captain of the carabinieri appeared and, after saluting me by bringing his right hand to the peak of his cap, said, 'It appears you are in danger, Il Duce. I have been ordered to ensure your safety.'" My father responded, "I don't think I'm in danger, but if you insist, please take a seat in my automobile."

18

The captain pointed instead to an ambulance that had entered the gardens of Villa Savoia. "You'll be safer in here," he said. So, surrounded by four carabinieri and two plainclothes police officers, my father was escorted into the vehicle. Alarmed, he turned toward the Villa Savoia entrance and saw that the king had been watching. Then, as the ambulance pulled away, he saw the king go back inside.

The coup, he only later realized, had been successfully executed by King Vittorio Emanuele III in the most painless manner. He subsequently learned that Chief of Police Clerici and General Castellano both knew what was to take place that afternoon. He also found out that the king had issued his arrest orders to General Ambrosio, who in turn passed them on to General Cerica, appointed commander of the Arma dei Carabinieri only a few days earlier.

CHAPTER 3

He Had a Plan for Ending the War

While my father's fate was being decided in Rome, I was on summer holiday in Riccione with my sister Anna Maria and sister-in-law Gina. Ola, my brother Vittorio's first wife, and Marcello Di Salvo, the son of a very dear friend of my mother's, were also with us.

Mamma remained home at Villa Torlonia, worried about the events she observed day by day coming to a head. She would telephone a few times a day to hear how we were and to ask us news about our vacation. I would tell her about my piano lessons with Marcello. He was another person who brought me to music. I learned to play by ear and never studied methodically. In contrast, my father had studied with Pietro Nenni while he was in prison at Forlì in 1911.

My mother called again on July 25, 1943. I remember that it was late afternoon, and I had been arguing with Ola about permission to go out with a young girl. It was to be my first date. I had carefully combed my hair and checked every detail in the mirror. But I was very upset because Ola wouldn't give me permission to go out.

So it was that when my mother called, I turned to her for help. From the sound of her voice, however, I immediately realized that something was wrong. "None of you may leave the house tonight," she said in the brusque tone she would assume in difficult moments. "Do you understand? No one can go out, not for any reason."

Why was my mother so worried? At the time, I thought it was because in Riccione there had been talk for several days about some English submarines being spotted in the Adriatic. I thought my mother had heard about them and was alarmed.

Even while reasoning through this, a premonition of sorts flashed through my mind. It was something I had never experienced before and would experience again only a few times over the course of my lifetime. I promised my mother I wouldn't go out. I hung up the receiver and called to Anna Maria. "It's terrible," I told her. "I think that someone is going to harm our father."

I later learned that at that same moment, the telephone rang at Villa Torlonia—the telephone was in the breakfast room, though my mother used to call it the small dining room attached to the kitchen. It is where she often spent her days. She picked up the receiver believing that it was me calling her right back. Instead, on the other end of the line she heard a male voice gasping, "Is this Donna Rachele?"

"Yes, it is. Who is this? What do you want from me?"

"They arrested Il Duce."

My mother stood frozen, as if she had turned to stone. For several moments she was incapable of uttering a single word. Then, finding her voice, she repeated, "Who are you? Tell me who you are. I want to know."

The hurried response came, "They arrested him just now, but there are people coming and I can't speak. Warn your children in Riccione to get out of harm's way."

"Your mother," Il Duce later revealed, "found herself feeling the same way she had twenty years earlier when, every so often, someone would approach her and tell her that I'd been arrested. I was a subversive in those days."

Mamma was extremely upset. Even Irma, her trusted housekeeper, couldn't calm her down. When she pulled herself together a little, she called Galbiati, the militia chief. It's difficult to believe, but he knew nothing. "Nothing has happened," he answered awkwardly. "Someone lied to you." In fact, something terrible had happened. A truck full of carabinieri had entered the Villa Torlonia gardens and the telephone line had suddenly gone silent.

"In the turmoil," my mother recounted, "I had forgotten about Vittorio. He had come home late the previous evening and spent a good part of the day in his room. Vittorio knew nothing about any of this, and I needed some time to explain what had happened. 'They've arrested your father,' I told him. 'Go at once and be safe.'"

Vittorio hesitated before obeying her. Then he went to the garage, took his methane-fueled Topolino, and left Villa Torlonia. In the streets, he told me, the people were screaming, "The war is over!"

In the meantime, I was so upset that Marcello, in an attempt to calm me down, told Gina that he would take me to the villa his family had rented, a short distance away, for a few hours. There we turned on the radio to listen to the latest news. We were thunderstruck, "The Cavaliere Benito Mussolini," the speaker announced, "resigned this morning."

In my naïveté, I didn't even dream that a lie could be hiding behind those words. I flew into a rage, "But how is this possible?" I kept repeating to Marcello. "How could it be true that my father would leave the government at a time like this? No, it's impossible. My father is not a coward!"

We rushed back to our holiday house in Riccione, where Gina and Ola told us that we were in danger because, following my father's resignation, there would be people who would wish us harm. We had to leave immediately and seek refuge with someone we could trust. Again, Marcello Di Salvo and his family came to the rescue, welcoming us into their home.

For the sake of complete historical accuracy, I must say that nothing bad happened to us. The agents assigned to surveillance remained at their posts, and no one threatened or bothered us.

The following morning I learned again from the radio that my father had been arrested at Villa Savoia. We asked one of the agents to buy the newspapers. To this day, those front pages are indelibly impressed in my memory.

There was one in particular that I recall with extreme clarity. *Il Gazzettino*, published in Venice on July 26, 1943, carried the following headline across all eight columns, printed in capital letters, on three lines, one above the other:

MUSSOLINI RESIGNS
KING TAKES CONTROL OF ARMED FORCES
BADOGLIO HEAD OF MILITARY GOVERNMENT

King Vittorio Emanuele III's and Field Marshal Pietro Badoglio's statements followed.

However, I do not wish to focus on these two individuals. For the first time, after so many years, I want to explain what actually occurred following my father's arrest. While getting rid of him for good would have been so simple, someone had decided that it was advisable to keep him alive. Killing my father would not have been advantageous for anyone. The truth, then, is that behind Il Duce's laborious and improvised changes of location, which began immediately after his arrest at Villa Savoia, a very important international game was being played out. It was a game in which the opposing sides, each convinced that they could use my father to achieve their own goals, thought it better not to eliminate him.

Badoglio was already looking forward to the moment when the war, which he pretended to believe in but knew was already lost, would end in capitulation. My father would then be handed over to the Allies, thus relieving Badoglio of an enormous responsibility and earning him valuable points with the Allies. As for the Germans, aside from Hitler's personal unwillingness to have my father killed, which he would demonstrate by stabbing my father in the back at his darkest hour, they preferred that he remain alive so as to lead the Italians who were still on their side.

Killing my father, I repeat, suited no one. Few are aware, however (and I have confirmed this with certainty, having consulted previously undisclosed documents), that my father's arrest on July 25th by the king prevented Il Duce from executing a sensational political maneuver he had studied on several occasions with his closest collaborators.

What was the maneuver in question? "In the midst of this darkness," my father would say, "I don't rule out the possibility of a final day of sunshine." Puzzling words, and ones he also addressed to his son-in-law Galeazzo Ciano on more than one occasion. In essence, Il Duce hoped to somehow extricate Italy from the war. This, in part, explains his strangely passive reaction when faced with the Grand Council's vote of no-confidence. He wanted to put his cards on the table with the Germans and reach an agreement about an independent plan of action for the common good before the situation grew worse with the involvement of the United States, a development whose devastating consequences he in fact intuited long before Hitler did.

SO, LET US RETURN to the ambulance that left Villa Savoia with my father on board and took him to the Victor Emanuele II School for Carabinieri in via Legnano. Here is what my mother, who, as always, maintained a meticulous record of events, later told us children: "A folding cot had been set up in the commander's office where your father stretched out, exhausted from the day's events. He was so pale and weak that a doctor was called in, a certain Dr. Santillo. They found his pulse to be very weak, but he refused treatment. He expressed a single request: to be permitted to shave, as he had neglected to do so that day despite his visit to the king. 'With this awful beard,' he said, 'I feel out of place.'"

My father remained in the school for two days, until 8 P.M. on July 27. To everyone it seemed he had disappeared into thin air. No one knew what had happened to him. Only later did we learn that this was a test of sorts, ordered by Badoglio, with the purpose of measuring how Il Duce's most faithful followers would react to his disappearance.

Badoglio put into action another piece of his plan by having General Ferone deliver the following letter to my father:

Your Excellency, Cavaliere Benito Mussolini,

The undersigned head of the government, having received specific evidence from several parties of a serious plot against your life, would like to inform you that the measures being taken are for your personal benefit and safety. Deeply regretting this turn of events, I would like to inform you that I am ready to issue orders to ensure your safe conduct to a location of your choosing.

Head of Government
Pietro Badoglio

My father consulted with General Ferone, who suggested that he request an escort to Rocca delle Caminate. Il Duce liked the idea and sent this response back to Badoglio:

I would like to thank you for the attention bestowed on me. I would also like to assure you that, remembering how we collaborated in the past, you

*can count on my complete cooperation. I am happy
to hear of the decision to continue the war with our
German allies, which is what the interests and honor
of our Homeland demand at this moment. As for
me, the only residence I have available is in Rocca
delle Caminate, where I may be transferred at any
moment.*

And so, at 8 P.M. on the night of July 27, 1943, following a day spent with no food in one of the rooms at
the school, my father was escorted to the courtyard of the
building. He was ushered into a dark automobile that
started for Via Flaminia and headed north, or so he
thought.

"As the vehicle sped through the dark," he told me,
"I realized that we had not taken Via Flaminia but Via
Appia. Badoglio had deceived me once again. Instead of
to Rocca, they were taking me to Gaeta, which we
reached at approximately two in the morning.

"The car I was in and the two other cars in escort
stopped at the pier named in honor of Costanzo Ciano, the
famous Fascist leader and Galeazzo's father. There, waiting with engines running was a gunboat, the *Persephone*.

"I was escorted from the car and climbed on board.
Several minutes later, the *Persephone* was at sea. I discovered that Saverio Polito, a police inspector who had
been in my service for a dozen years in Riccione, was
assigned to me. He told me that two days earlier he had
been named head of the military police."

CHAPTER 4

The Mysteries of Gran Sasso

I personally knew two of the three German officers who freed my father from Campo Imperatore on Gran Sasso in September 1943—SS Captain Otto Skorzeny and Wehrmacht Captain Hans Mors. I heard about the third, Gerhardt Martens, from his son Oliver, who lives in Monaco.

Skorzeny coordinated the operation, which the Führer himself had ordered. Mors commanded the contingent of paratroopers involved in the blitz, twenty to arrive at Campo Imperatore by air and forty more by cable car. Martens was the man for impossible missions —charged with piloting the small Fieseler Storch, a reconnaissance "Stork" plane that was to carry my father from Campo Imperatore to Vienna. Lieutenant Heinrich Gerlach, another young ace pilot, rounded out the commando unit.

For more than sixty years, my father's liberation from Gran Sasso was attributed solely to Skorzeny, even though Mors and Martens played crucial roles. Before reconstructing the actual events, however, allow me to take a few steps back and pose a question: Why was my father not killed during the imprisonment following his arrest on July 25, 1943?

Herein lies the answer. My father arrived on the island of Ponza on July 28 aboard the *Persephone* and remained there for only a few days. The new head of the Italian government, Pietro Badoglio, worried that the Germans would stage a surprise attack and attempt to free him. However, Hitler feared that the Americans might kidnap him. Both hypotheses were plausible, especially given the fact that the garrison on Ponza was small and poorly armed.

"And so it was that on August 7," my father told my mother and me, "I was taken on board the *Panthère,* a French navy unit, and moved to La Maddalena on Sardinia, where a well-armed naval base was located. I stayed in a small house surrounded by armed men. In the living room, lined up on a shelf, were the twenty-two volumes of Nietzsche's complete works that Hitler had sent me for my sixty-first birthday on July 29. They were late in arriving at Ponza. I was very pleased with this gift but was already forced to part with it on the 28th of August. From La Maddalena, I was taken by hydroplane to Lake Bracciano, where an ambulance was waiting for me—the same ambulance that had taken me from Villa Savoia on July 25."

It was on July 25 that several carabinieri escorted Il Duce and told him they would accompany him first to Rome and then to Rocca delle Caminate. "There you can see your wife and children again," they added. The ambulance did, in truth, head for the capital. But rather than enter the city, it turned onto Via Sabina, changing direction toward Abruzzo. At Campo Imperatore (2,112 meters above sea level), there was a large hotel near the cable car landing. It was here that Badoglio wanted my father held.

Thus we arrive at the first mystery. On the 28th of July, there were so many tourists at the hotel that there was no room for the prisoner, so instead he had to be detained in an annex downhill, near the cable car starting point. I speak of a mystery because it seems hard to believe that the hotel was not cleared prior to Il Duce's arrival. There's only one explanation for this—my father had to be at Campo Imperatore and nowhere else precisely on September 12 in order to make the German rescue possible. His rescue had to have been in coordination with a plan already meticulously worked out and that involved Hitler's direct participation.

Was Badoglio involved in the scheme? I don't exclude the possibility. The alternative is that someone very important was influencing his decisions, placing him within reach of German counterintelligence. One thing remains certain. The twenty carabinieri under Lieutenant Scaiola's command who held my father in custody hadn't the slightest idea about what was to take place.

"On September 4," my father told me, "I was transferred from the annex to the hotel, which by then had been cleared of tourists. On the evening of the 8th, after the armistice was announced over the radio, I noticed that surveillance around the hotel had been reinforced. On the 10th, by chance I intercepted a news item on the radio announcing that one of the conditions of the armistice was my handover to the Allies. I vowed I would not be taken alive and I wrote as much in a letter that I gave to Lieutenant Scaiola. The poor man rushed to my room, distraught, and removed anything that might be used by me in an act of despair. Later, crying, he told me that he would never hand an Italian over to the English, the same people who had already held him prisoner."

On September 12 at two o'clock in the afternoon, following a light meal, my father stood at the window of his room, which overlooked a ravine. "Suddenly, a glider floated in a hundred meters from the hotel with a silent weightlessness," he described. "And before I could even stop to wonder where it had come from, I saw several men in uniform advance. At first I thought they were English, but then, relieved, I recognized their German uniforms. They moved quickly and pointed some machine guns in the direction of the hotel."

Before continuing with the story, I want to introduce some important background information. The decision to rescue my father had been made on July 26 when Hitler called Otto Skorzeny to his headquarters in eastern Prussia. On this occasion, the Führer entrusted the SS captain with another charge—to make an example of and to punish all those responsible for Il Duce's downfall: first, the Savoia royal family, then Badoglio and all the other members of his government. To fulfill his dual mission, Skorzeny was given carte blanche permission to use any means necessary. In addition, the Führer informed him that he would have at his disposal General Kurt Student's paratroopers and the SS Leibstandarte division stationed near Rome.

While the blitz on Campo Imperatore and Il Duce's liberation was an unqualified victory for Skorzeny, with

Mors and Martens at his side, punishing the architects of the July 25 no-confidence vote against my father was a more limited success. The only Savoia royalty the captain was able to deliver to Hitler was Princess Mafalda, lured into a trap on September 22. The unfortunate daughter of King Victor Emanuele III was told that if she turned herself in to the German command in Rome, she would be flown to Germany to join her husband, Filippo d'Assia, and their four children. Naturally, she accepted. But instead of landing in Berlin, the plane took her directly to Buchenwald death camp, where she died several months later.

Returning now to the commando raid at Campo Imperatore, as my father described it, "More gliders were landing on the plateau opposite the hotel, about ten in total. As armed men descended from the craft, I heard a great noise in the hotel. I heard orders being given in Italian and in German. At a certain point, I realized too that other German soldiers were reaching the hotel by cable car to take part in the operation begun by their fellow soldiers, the ones I could see from my window."

From his vantage point, my father had an accurate view of events. To be exact, nine gliders (another two had remained on the ground, damaged) had taken off from the Pratica di Mare Airport and had been towed to cruising altitude by as many motored aircraft. As I said, about twenty paratroopers landed at Campo Imperatore, while another forty arrived by land via cable car. Coordinating the two separate contingents, which together overwhelmed the defenders at the hotel, was Captain Mors.

By my father's account, "The German groups were advancing so quickly that the carabinieri didn't have time to react, assuming they even wanted to. I heard the click of gun cartridges being loaded inside the hotel. Any moment now, I'm thinking, the rifles will start firing. Then I approached the window and yelled, 'Can't you see that there's an Italian general!' And truly, clearly sticking out from among the German paratroopers nearest the hotel was the gray-green uniform of an Italian general. I had seen him on several occasions. His name was Soleti and he had been taken hostage that morning in preparation for the raid."

The reality is that not a single shot was fired. And this is the second mystery of Campo Imperatore. Had the carabinieri received orders not to respond to the German attack? Or perhaps they didn't open fire so as not to put my father's life in danger given that the armistice required he be handed over to the Allies alive? No one knew then, as no one knows today. Not even my father knew, who said, "Perhaps my pointing out General Soleti was what averted the gunfire. That is, at least, what I believe. And that is what Captain Skorzeny said to me when he burst into my room, out of breath and exultant, while conveying Hitler's regards and solidarity."

I'VE SAID THAT the operation's success was largely due to the talents of Captain Mors, who not only coordinated the raid, but had the idea of capturing General Soleti. There's no doubt that the latter was an important tactical move. If nothing else, seeing the high-ranking Italian officer among the Germans confused the carabinieri and so they took no action. None of Skorzeny's men opened fire on the Italian carabinieri, demonstrating their true nerves of steel and excellent training. During the course of the entire operation, there was but a single injury—a German paratrooper slipped and fell hard against a boulder.

Many years later, when I met Skorzeny in Madrid, he acknowledged the significance of Mors' idea to capture General Soleti. "To show his gratitude," he told me, "Il Duce invited Mors to Gargnano during the six hundred days of the Salò Republic."

My father didn't tell me whether it was Gerlach or Martens who piloted the Stork aircraft. I'm inclined to believe it was the latter, trusting what his son Oliver said to me shortly after his father's death on March 9, 2003.

Gerhardt Otto Wilhelm Martens was born into a well-to-do family in Hamburg on December 14, 1919. At age 19, he left the luxurious family residence on the banks of the river Elba and enlisted in the air force. In a short time, he became one of the youngest instructor pilots in the Third Reich.

Martens was an ace pilot of light aircraft, which led him to play a key role on the Russian front. His notable talent meant that he was repeatedly sent into areas controlled by the Red Army in order to rescue German prisoners of war. It is more than plausible that Skorzeny, who needed an exceptional pilot to rescue my father in a light airplane, thought of him.

Martens was a rigorous and uncompromising military man who always maintained maximum confidentiality about the missions with which he had been entrusted, even with his family. His son, Oliver, has a collection of his father's personal belongings as well as photographs of some of the aircraft he flew. One photograph features the famous Stork used by the Skorzeny group at Gran Sasso.

AND NOW WE ARRIVE at the final stage of the raid. More than sixty years have passed, but the dramatic force of that moment remains fully intact for me to this day because my father had never been so close to death.

"We had to leave Campo Imperatore as quickly as possible," he recounted, "but we found ourselves facing a final, unexpected obstacle. Skorzeny, who was a giant of a man, insisted at all costs on squeezing into the narrow cabin of the Stork. It had landed on the plateau along with the gliders, but the makeshift runway was truly minute and the pilot said that we couldn't take off with Skorzeny's extra ninety kilos on board. Skorzeny then demanded that we get off the plane and help him move it back a few meters in order to extend the runway for takeoff.

"I remember that it was three o'clock sharp on September 12 when the little plane started taxiing. It sped over the stony strip of land and I saw a ravine approaching quickly, the aircraft still not having lifted off the ground. I think there was less than a meter left before the abyss when the pilot finally managed to raise the nose of the plane. I heard the Germans and the Italians yelling. The fact that the Stork, as heavily loaded as it was, didn't plummet into the ravine was something of a miracle.

"I turned to look back, and on the plateau, which was still just below us, I saw many arms waving. Later, as if to seal this remarkable event in my memory, the image on the ground was replaced by the profound silence of the upper atmosphere. After a few minutes, we were flying over Aquila. An hour later, the Stork landed at Pratica di Mare."

Twenty hours later, at the airport in Monaco, a military aircraft brought my father to see my mother, my sister Anna Maria, and me. Never has an embrace been stronger or more moving.

CHAPTER 5

Five Letters for an Entire Lifetime

Some time between 1946 and 1957, my mother received a parcel from Rome accompanied by a letter signed by Italian Undersecretary of State Giulio Andreotti. At her request, I opened the package and read to her the enclosed note:

> *Dearest Signora,*
>
> *In reorganizing the Presidency archives, some letters were found which belonged to your husband and pertain exclusively to family matters. It seems right that these handwritten notes be returned to the family, and I, therefore, consider myself obliged to forward them to you.*
>
> *With sincerest regards,*
> *Giulio Andreotti*

Every time my mother wanted to relive the years she spent with my father, she would leaf through the letters from Il Duce which Giulio Andreotti had returned to her. There were five, the only ones that remained of their entire correspondence. In fact, all of the letters she brought with her when she left Gargnano and then hid at Lago di Como before being arrested with Anna Maria and me on April 29, 1945, had disappeared. She no longer even had my father's final letter, which he wrote two days before being killed.

These five letters are, in a sense, my father's hand-written testimony. They were written in red and blue ink, as was his habit. All five pertain to the days following his arrest at Villa Savoia, on July 25, 1943, when he was taken to the island of Ponza and later to La Maddalena. The first letter, dated July 30, 1943, reads as follows:

> *Dear Rachele,*
>
> *Thank you for the items you sent me, and above all for the pictures of our loved ones. Bruno has been in my thoughts these days, on his second, sad anniversary.*
>
> *Regards from me to Vittorio, Edda, Romano, Anna, and everyone. I am calm and patient. I'd like to add that I am being treated with the utmost respect. I send you much love on the first day of my sixty-first year.*
>
> *Yours,*
> *Benito*

Fourteen days passed and my father, who had been moved from Ponza to La Maddalena, which, according to Badoglio was easier to defend in the event of any attempts to liberate Il Duce, received a letter from my mother giving him family news. He responded like this:

Dear Rachele,

I received your letter, the second in twenty days, and I see that you are in Rocca with everyone, except Vittorio. I, too, know nothing of his whereabouts, and I hope you hear from him soon.

My health is fairly good, my conscience clear. I have worked for twenty years, without rest, unselfishly, with complete loyalty. You know better than anyone how I have fought for the people.

On the anniversary of Bruno's death, I had a mass read, but I could not attend. I hope that you were permitted to remember our Bruno, who today is dead and whose soul must truly be tormented.

I've been living in complete isolation for twenty days now. I only receive the Italian and German war bulletins. I ignore everything, and besides, I don't know what I have become. How did you leave Villa Torlonia? What has happened with I Pòpolo d'Italia? How is Anna?

Don't worry about food and laundry. Regards from me to everyone, to the children, to Gina, Marina, and the trusty house servants.

I too am waiting to see what happens.

Love,

Your Benito

My father wrote the third letter to my mother on August 15, after he received a missive in which my mother had asked about his health, what he thought would happen, and in particular, where he hoped to convince his wardens to take him:

Dear Rachele,

On the evening of July 25, I was asked which residence I preferred, where I wish to be accompanied. I chose Rocca. But General Polito told me that my arrival in Rocca would incite hostility from the residents of Forli and is, therefore, not a possibility. As I do not wish to have a raid or even a simple alarm attributed to my presence in Rocca, I have decided to abandon the idea, at least for the time being. I regret the decision very much because I wanted to see you again, see all of you again, but I believe that my decision will help to keep the peace.

I've requested news of Vittorio from di Vito and his secretary De Cesare on my personal stationery, but I still have not received any. As soon as I learn anything, I will let you know. In all, I have received two letters from you and a telegram from Göring. They also give me the Italian and German war bulletins. Of the two books you sent me, I gave one as a gift to a priest, and the other, Carducci's poetry, to an officer.

I won't talk to you about my health, nor of the physical conditions. All this has scarcely had any importance in my life. Now it has none. Morally I am at ease, because my conscience is clear. I don't know what will happen to me. I beg you to prepare Romano and Anna for life, especially Anna. Kiss everyone for me. And for you an affectionate embrace from your Benito.

My father was being deceived by General Polito, who, completely without foundation, told him that his arrival in Rocca delle Caminate would be badly received by local residents. The reality was entirely different, but Il Duce had no way of knowing this and thus decided against going to Rocca.

When my mother realized this deception had taken place, she flew into a rage. She remembered Polito, the ex-constable of Bologna, as "a servile official" for whom carrying her bags was an honor and who now sought to profit from Il Duce's situation.

On August 2, 1943, Polito asked my mother to leave Villa Torlonia and move to Rocca, assuring her that her children would be there as well. My mother first placed Il Duce's medals, which she didn't want to part with, in a small army locker. Then she spent a long while walking through the whole house. "My sons and daughters came here as small children," she wrote in her diary, "and they are leaving as adults, ready to start their own families. This is where I said good-bye to Bruno for the last time, who Destiny took from me so early. Here, after so many years of happiness, I also spent the sad days of war. The words of several loyal officers further intensified my emotions and I felt a void opening up in me."

She left for Rocca the evening of August 2nd at around eleven o'clock. My mother said that Polito continually smoked a cigar inside the car. With the windows tightly shut, it was suffocating. When he got out, he would make her stay inside the car, as if she presented a threat.

Little by little, as the drive continued, he revealed his true self by cruelly insisting on the darkest predictions for Il Duce's fate. He then did something that infuriated my mother and frightened her. He began to make romantic advances toward her and put his hands on her. Coming from this scoundrel, this was just another way to humiliate my mother and, in so doing, to strike at Il Duce.

Here's the letter my father wrote on August 19:

Dear Rachele,

Today I received your letter from the 13th of this month. You should have received another one from me in the meantime. Don't worry about the books. From Field Marshall Göring, I received a sculpture as a gift, but the Führer sent me a case with twenty two magnificently bound volumes. I see that you are lonely, too. I would never have believed that our fellow countrymen would so quickly reveal themselves. Another illusion! Patience.

I have received official notice that Vittorio has gone abroad and, as a result, been declared a deserter. This is a great disappointment to me. Maybe he felt he was in danger. As far as work is concerned, I know nothing, but I think that things will slowly fall into place. As for the Genoese children I evacuated to Carpena and sponsored through June, leave them be. Someone else will provide for them or for their exodus.

Affectionately yours,
Benito

The letter ended with three postscripts in red. The first was addressed to my cousin Vito, the second to me, and the third to my sister Anna Maria. Here they are:

Dear Vito,

I've received official notification that you're in Rocca because you were advised against going to Milan. This leads me to suppose that Il Popolo d'Italia will be suppressed and destroyed. Don't worry. Love, your uncle.

Dear Romanuzzo,

How do you spend your time between alarms? Have you decided what to study at university? We'll discuss it again.

Dear Anna,

Tell me how you are and whether the professor is still taking care of your health. This storm will also pass and perhaps won't even be the last in my lifetime. I love you all very much.

We realized then that not only was my father being kept completely in the dark and my mother's letters censored, but that he was receiving erroneous information in order to stir his agony and destroy his morale. It was completely false that Vittorio had been declared a deserter and it was also a lie that the residents of Forlì were hostile to Il Duce's arrival at Rocca.

The last of the five letters had to do with what my mother had communicated to Il Duce using a sort of coded language to avoid censure. He understood that the residents of Forlì bore no hostility toward him, but he still had doubts about my brother Vittorio's fate. In fact, not even my mother knew that my brother was in Germany, where he had gone in the hopes of organizing Il Duce's release:

Dear Rachele,

I received your note of August 24 from Commander Gueli, and he is kind enough to bring you mine. I've already told you that I have changed residences again. As for Vito, I learned he was in Rocca from the police, via the admiral. Now I'll ask again. I know that Il Popolo d'Italia is no longer being published. Above all, I'm happy to hear what you tell me about the local situation. It was completely ungrateful for me to think that everything I'd done in the past twenty years has been completely forgotten.

Since you insist on knowing about the condition of my health, I will tell you that it is stable but slowly deteriorating. However, this is of absolutely no importance to me.

Once again the letter ended with a postscript for me and one for Anna Maria. In the one addressed to me, Papà responds to greetings I had sent in my mother's last letter:

Dear Romano,

Thank you for your short note, much as it was telegraphic. Don't worry. We'll think about schools when the time comes.

The postscript for Anna read as follows:

I'm glad to hear that you are dealing with the situation with a "strong spirit." That's good. Take care of your health. And Gina, what is she doing? And Martina? Give my regards to everyone. Benito M.

It was the first time he signed his letter "Benito M." The letter was not dated, which led us to believe that Il Duce had been moved yet again. In reality, after being kept on the island for twenty days, on August 28, 1943, he was taken to Gran Sasso, and to the Campo Imperatore Hotel from which the German paratroopers would later rescue him. But that's a story you already know.

CHAPTER 6

My Mother Meets Claretta Petacci

Even today many people ask me when my family came to know about my father's relationship with Claretta Petacci. Everyone is curious about how my mother reacted.

I was the first in the family to face the affair in early June 1943. I know it's difficult to believe, but it's true. Until that time, my mother had always turned a blind eye to a reality everyone knew of but she evidently tried in every way to suppress.

Villa Torlonia had a large atrium opening directly to the back of a Doric column supporting the tympanum on the building's facade. It was a vast space paved in marble at the center of which a large silver platter, designated for collecting the mail, stood on a tripod. The platter commemorated Italy's victory at the 1934 World Soccer Championship, an heirloom Vittorio and I would have very much liked to come into our possession, especially my brother, who was a great fan of the sport.

Collected in the platter were envelopes addressed to my father (generally petitions for his assistance), my mother, and us children. Looking back on it today, as accustomed as we are to a world in which threats and danger abound, I'm amazed at the detached tranquility with which those in charge of security permitted these letters to be delivered in person, directly into the heart of Villa Torlonia. In fact, strangers could gain access to the private residence of the head of the Fascist government simply by presenting their identification. Who could have known whether their intentions were hostile?

Packages and small boxes were often delivered along with the letters, and anyone could have placed whatever they desired—from a letter bomb to a real bomb—on this large plate that bore the signatures of the world champion soccer players. I remember that we received a wide-ranging assortment of souvenirs: from an alpine star addressed to my mother to a bottle of special wine that a faithful supporter from Romagna hoped to have my father try. In short, there was absolutely no filter. But, thank heaven, we never met with any harm.

In June of 1943, a letter addressed "To Signor Romano Mussolini" appeared on the platter. It was an anonymous letter containing a revelation that left me breathless—a woman, Claretta Petacci, had for some time been my father's lover. And, in order for me to be able to recognize her, the anonymous writer included a detailed description, including her age, build, eye color, and hair color. Then it continued with an account of her visits to Palazzo Venezia, which took place in the afternoon ("every afternoon," it specified) and lasted "anywhere from fifteen minutes to two hours."

A vivid image provided the closing: "This beautiful, young woman goes to Palazzo Venezia and enters Il Duce's study without anyone having to accompany her. She usually wears a dust coat over her dress because she arrives on her motorcycle with a sidecar."

As soon as I finished reading this letter, I quickly folded up the piece of paper. It was burning a hole through my hands and I didn't know what to do with it. As I was getting ready for school, I threw it in my bag and went out. I intended to show the letter to Vittorio once I came home. On the way, however, I changed my mind, crumpled it up, and threw it away.

It seemed impossible to me that my mother didn't know. In thinking about it, however, I reached the conclusion that if she did know, it could not have been for long, not for more than one month, since that was how much time had passed from a conversation we'd had whose significance I didn't realize at the time, but that now came back to me in a new light. "Your father," she said, "may have all the failings in the world, but he's a good husband who has never spent a night away from home. Who knows why some people want to plant a seed of distrust in my ear. But it's labor lost. I pay no mind to gossip but hold to the facts."

I remember, incidentally, that even after learning of the affair with Claretta Petacci, my mother made every possible excuse for my father. "In so many years," she said, "he never let us—you children or me—want for anything. He was an affectionate father and husband. And, above all, he never once allowed that woman to come into contact with any of us."

There was another quality of his to which my mother gave great importance. Up to the very end, and she was very clear on this matter, my father had fulfilled his conjugal duties.

Poor Mamma! I still remember the expression on her face when she read the newspapers following Il Duce's arrest. Free of the binds of censorship as well as good taste, they openly exaggerated all the details of the Mussolini and Petacci love affair.

In my mother's eyes, I saw sadness and loss. She told me, "I was torn to pieces with jealousy over this woman, so much younger than me.... but, more than anything, I worried that this time your father and I would not have the opportunity to reconcile. We had done so on many other occasions. You know, don't think that I was blind or stupid. When your father's mind was elsewhere, I knew it."

Clearly, as her son, I could do nothing but show solidarity with my mother. As time passed, however, I understood that "that woman's" tie to my father was very strong, as later their terrible deaths in 1945 would demonstrate to the whole world.

That man and that woman, so alone in the face of events so large, come back into my mind at the strangest moments. It happened even recently when I was playing with my band at Lago di Garda. To reach the venue, I passed by Villa Fiordaliso in Gargnano, the "house of the dead" in which Claretta Petacci stayed during the period of the Republic of Salò. The building awoke in me a series of burning memories. It reminded me of my mother's meeting with Claretta and the ensuing drama immediately following, which very nearly ended in tragedy.

Here we are in 1943 again. Virtually everything had been compromised and the situation was getting worse.

After July 25, Claretta was also imprisoned. When she was released, she could have fled. Any other woman in her place would have done so, but she didn't. She was so devoted that she managed to find a residence in Gargnano at Lago di Garda, only a few hundred meters away from the home of the man for whom she lived. The fact that this was also the home of my mother said little for her tact. But given a love that could not be broken even by the threat of death (because this is exactly what she faced), even the provocation of proximity to my mother became, in some way, acceptable.

I admit that I felt a sort of tenderness for Claretta Petacci, a feeling that my brother Vittorio also shared. I make sense of this knowing that I would never have dared judge my father's choices or interfere in his decisions. He defended his relationship with Claretta so resolutely that I assumed there had to have been something of greater consequence between them than physical attraction, in his soul as well as in hers, for she was devoted to him to the point of sacrificing her life for him without any hesitation.

To be sure, though less widely known because they took place during the years when he was in power, there were other relationships that were important to my father such as that with the writer Margherita Sarfatti. She had a tremendous influence on him, but their relationship did not cause my mother as much suffering as the one with Claretta.

"I knew about Margherita Sarfatti, and I was furious," Mamma admitted. "But I wasn't threatened by her because I knew your father would return to me. With

Petacci, however, I felt powerless. It hurt me to have to admit that she had a place in your father's mind and that she could have stolen him from me forever."

In Gargnano on Lago di Garda, however, the situation quickly became untenable. Claretta's close presence, observed by many, put my mother in a state of continuous agitation.

These are her words: "I knew she was residing on the lake, but I didn't know where precisely. It was only by accident, during a visit with relatives of Bruno's widow, that I discovered where this woman was staying.

"My first impulse, naturally, was to go and confront her. Later I reconsidered, concluding that it might imperil your father, who was already in grave danger because of his relationship with that woman. In fact, I knew she wasn't there by chance. She had been placed there with a very specific objective—to keep an eye on Il Duce and report on his plans. Her house was full of wires and strange boxes."

My mother put Il Duce's back to the wall. If he didn't end things immediately with Claretta Petacci, she would be the one to chase her out of Gargnano. My father acquiesced and told her he would break things off. He added that in the time we had been on the lake, he had seen her only once, and only in order to end things.

I suffered as I listened to my parents fight. My mother was resolute and furious; my father, however, exhibited a fatalistic resignation that frightened me. He no longer seemed himself.

During the subsequent meeting with Claretta—I can't say whether it was the "only meeting," as he insisted—he was accompanied by General Wolff, charged by Hitler to stay close to him. Wolff, like my mother, was convinced that Claretta was a threat to my father and that they needed to be separated. A new destination had already been selected for her, a castle near Trento where she could be joined by her family.

A week passed. What was happening in our private lives was eclipsed by everything else going on around us, especially the bombing of the big cities where the dead numbered in the thousands. Everything in our family moved to the background. Despite this, the worm of jealousy and, above all, her unbearable humiliation would not give my mother peace. When she realized that my father had not kept his word, she decided to take action.

I saw her leaving Villa Feltrinelli with a pained expression. If I had had the power to prevent her from meeting with Claretta, I confess I would have exercised it. But I was a nervous and frightened teenager who empathized with my mother's suffering but also with my father's interests.

Mamma summoned her driver and asked him to take her to Villa Fiordaliso. "It was dark and it was raining," she told me. "A good while after I had rung the bell and called out, the gate was opened by a German officer who, judging by his embarrassment, must have been alerted to my arrival. 'Are you armed?' he asked me. I replied that I was not, that I didn't need weapons in order to confront her. He led me into the villa where an old woman then took me by the arm and showed me into a small room."

These are my mother's words: "The blood was pulsating at my temples and when that woman entered the room, my heart stopped for a moment. She was holding a voile handkerchief in her hands, like an old chanteuse, and it had a strange effect on me. I never could have imagined it. She seemed helpless, like a fragile plant. Only afterward did I realize that at that moment I had allowed myself to be disarmed by her. Later on, I couldn't forget the terrible anguish that overcame me."

The two rivals stood face-to-face. There are multiple accounts of their encounter, some of which are decidedly romanticized. The following are the essential points of their exchange.

"My husband needs peace," my mother began. "And people can't stand that you have come to live here. If what you are going to say is true—in short, that you love him—then for his sake, step back. Even I, his wife, would do so if it could help him. Stop seeing him. Leave here."

Claretta made no response. She covered her face with her handkerchief and cried. My mother, exasperated, reproached her, "Don't play innocent! You have had a telephone cable installed between this house and mine. What's more, you've stored in Germany some of Il Duce's compromising letters. You do not love him. You are his worst enemy."

Claretta continued to cry.

"Answer me!" my mother yelled. "Put an end to this disgusting performance!"

It was only when my mother grabbed her by the arms and started to shake her that Claretta decided to speak.

"You are a fortunate woman," she said. "Il Duce loves you very much, and I have never once dared say a single word against you."

My mother, caught by surprise, let go of her. Claretta then left the room and ran up to the floor above. When she reappeared, she was holding a bundle of letters in her hands. "These are thirty-two letters that your husband wrote to me. I am giving them to you because I am not a blackmailer."

My mother expected something of the sort. A single glance was enough to determine that those letters were not the originals, but typed copies. This young woman who stood before her in tears, this "fragile plant" who had thrown her off guard, was in reality controlling the game and now held her in check.

At that point, with my mother beside herself with rage, the conversation proceeded in a single direction— Mamma yelled and Claretta cried. Just as a German officer came into the room, Claretta fell to her knees and fainted on the floor.

"My head was burning," my mother told me. "And my heart was pounding. Turning back from the gates of the villa, I yelled, 'You'll get what you deserve, Signora!'"

Mother left feeling vanquished. She felt that she had lost her husband. In any case, she realized that no one could have succeeded in distancing him from that woman.

Upon returning to Villa Feltrinellli, she committed a desperate act. She locked herself in the bathroom, took a bottle of bleach from the cabinet and drank some of it.

"I don't know how much," she later confessed. "I only remember that I immediately felt very ill and, as I was fainting, realized that someone had forced the door open and was coming into the bathroom."

It was a maid who came to my mother's rescue and saved her life by forcing her to vomit and perhaps drink some milk, as we waited for the doctor to arrive. It was several more hours before Mamma took hold of herself. During that time, my father, who had been apprised of what happened, called at least ten times to hear how she was doing.

"He didn't have the courage to come to me," my mother later told me, "despite the fact that he was consumed with fear of losing me. At a certain point, he sent me a note which moved me. With great humility, he asked if I wanted to see him. I responded that I did, and he came to me only a few minutes later. He stayed with me all night, speaking to me softly and begging me to forgive him. That's the kind of man your father was."

CHAPTER 7

With My Father at Villa Carpena

My mother fulfilled an old wish of hers when, using her husband's first earnings as the editor of Avanti, she purchased Villa Carpena. This family residence, a few kilometers from Forlì, was the setting for many important events for us. Encircled by a spacious park and in part maintained as a garden to this day, the building itself was restored as a museum in 2002 and is now home to many of my father's personal effects. It also has many of the original furnishings that we were able to recover after they had been confiscated or plundered at the end of the war.

Villa Carpena bears a special meaning for me, not only because I was born there, but because this is where my mother lived out her last days.

Before sharing some of my memories of time spent there with my father, I would like to add a few words about this place. Villa Carpena is located only a short distance from Varano dei Costa, where my father was born on July 29, 1883, to Alessandro Mussolini and Rosa Maltoni in an old cottage resting on a small knoll in the village of Dovia. It was there that my grandfather had a blacksmith shop.

For the Mussolinis, therefore, in addition to being

home to many memories, Villa Carpena represents a spiritual landscape. It is here that our thoughts return at crucial moments in life, as if in search of a safe landing to ease our minds.

I must say that after the end of the war many politicians acted kindly toward us. Einaudi and De Gasperi, in particular, arranged for all of my mother's belongings to be returned to her. Among the items that came back into our possession, the one that bore the greatest material and emotional value to us, was Villa Carpena.

The building was occupied by several displaced families, so at first we had to adjust to living in the garage. Little by little, however, we managed to reclaim a good portion of the old furnishings and return the residence to its original condition. On certain days, small groups of people would congregate at the villa's gates. They had come to return paintings and furniture that came into their possession, often purchased from those who had stolen them. Some came from far away and often wouldn't reveal their real names. They would simply give us what they had brought, ask to kiss my mother's hand, and leave proudly.

Mamma eventually reclaimed full possession of Villa Carpena, and she wouldn't abandon it again until October 30, 1979, the day she passed away in the large, dark wooden bed that can still be seen in the restored museum. As for me, after she passed away, I could no longer sleep in the house. At first, I stayed with my cousin Romana Moschi and her husband, Nino. Today, when I go to nearby Predappio, I stay in a hotel.

Many people want to know what I've saved that

belonged to my father. Unfortunately, other than the museum objects and relics found in Villa Carpena, the answer is, very little. The most important remnant is an oil portrait depicting him in civilian clothes, sitting behind his desk in the large Sala del Mappamondo. About twenty years ago, from my savings, I was able to purchase the beautiful, large tapestry that was hung from the balcony of the Palazzo Venezia when Il Duce gave speeches. I had always admired this artwork, and I even had restored its silver fasces with the bay laurel crown in the center. With much regret, I have to say that the tapestry is no longer in my possession because I was forced to sell it.

I WAS FIVE YEARS OLD when my father told me the story of his life for the first time, right in the garden of Villa Carpena. He recalled the years of his childhood, as my siblings and I listened. Vittorio was sixteen years old, Bruno was fourteen, and Anna had just turned three. Our father spoke very simply, as he always did. However, he had a special way of infusing the most common words with solemnity so that in listening to him, one had the sensation of witnessing something important. All great speakers have this gift. What's more, as his children, we naturally considered him to be a superior being and hung on his every word, conscious that he was trying to impart as much of himself and his thoughts as possible, on that day in particular, his memories of childhood.

He would say, "I'm searching through my most distant memories to see myself again as a child. It's not easy because much time has passed, but something is coming back into my mind as if I were watching an old movie. Here's the first scene: I'm five years old and your Nonna Rosa is there, taking me in her arms, patting me gently on the back to help me stop coughing .... see how worried poor Nonna is. She still doesn't know that I have whooping cough."

At this point he would pause, allowing what he had been saying to sink into our minds, making us more curious about what was to come. Since I was five years old at the time, the same age as he was when he had whooping cough, I couldn't take my eyes off him. I felt that we were alike in some way, and he, sensing what I was feeling, looked at me affectionately with an expression that is still burned in my memory. He smiled and continued, "As soon as I recovered from whooping cough, I began to read primers. I was no prodigy, but I could make my way and Nonna Rosa was very proud of me."

I nodded. I was starting to work on the primers too, at the same age he had. I said this silently to myself, but he seemed to read my mind and, almost as if to comfort me about the difficulties I was having on my first encounter with consonants and vowels, consoled, "But don't worry too much, children, because in no time I learned to read and write properly."

From six to nine years of age, my father went to school, first as his mother's student, she was a teacher, and later as a student of Silvio Marani's. Nonna Rosa, in fact, taught first and second grade in Predappio, while Master Marani took over from the third grade.

While speaking to us, my father would cross his

arms, his famous black eyes wide open. He would then give us the impression that some discouragement was imminent. In reality, the disappointment he emoted was directed at himself. "You should know," he explained, "that I was a feisty and pugnacious rascal. More than once, I came home with my head cracked open by a stone, each time throwing my mother and grandmother, both of whom adored me, into a state of alarm."

I don't remember any more of Il Duce's first talk with us children. However, I have since been able to piece the rest together by reading the annotations published in his many books. On the subject of blows to the head, my father continued, "They hurt a great deal. But have no doubt, I knew how to get my revenge.

"On vacation days, I would grab a small shovel and, along with my brother Arnaldo, spend time playing in the gravel bed of the river. I was also a very bold country thief. I once stole some decoy pigeons and, pursued by their owner, frantically ran all the way up a hill. I remember too that I had to wade across a river to get away from him, but I wouldn't abandon my prey."

How distant that time seems now, how remote that hill and that river. Yet in my mind, their outline remains quite clear, like everything my father talked about—that is, both my father and my mother, to be precise— because many times it would fall on my mother to finish my father's stories, since he would unexpectedly be interrupted and have to leave in the middle of a story in order to attend to his responsibilities.

I can even imagine the moment my father was born. I always see in my mind's eye the blinding light of that

Sunday when he came into this world at two o'clock in the afternoon in the farmhouse in Dovia. He was born in a room with a brick floor, in the corner of which stood a double bed with a wrought iron headboard.

"It was in that bed, flanked by two small dark wooden dressers and a small stand with a mirror on it," Il Duce described, "that your Nonna Rosa brought me into the world. She was a great woman, remember this, who feared nothing and no one. I've already told you that she was my first teacher, and later she also taught my brother Arnaldo and my sister Edvige. But, children, do you know why there was a mirror on that small stand that stood next to the bed?"

My siblings and I were quiet at this point. Vittorio and Bruno were smiling because they had already heard the story. I, however, waited anxiously because I didn't know the answer to my father's question.

Can you imagine Il Duce with his fists at his sides, in the same pose he would assume in the coming years during crucial moments when he addressed the crowds from the balcony of Palazzo Venezia? Just like that—frozen in that position, somewhere between the serious and the comical—my father held an aura of mystery, mesmerizing to my child's eyes.

On large and small occasions, he knew how to keep his audience in suspense, which, in this instance, came to an end only when he finally explained, "My mother had no one to assist her during labor. So, first she had to do everything on her own, even check the mirror to see what point her paleness had reached from her labor pains. Only when the pain had become unbearable did she feel she needed to ask for help. And do you know how she did it? Calmly, without getting excited, modulating her tone of voice in order not to alarm my father, 'My husband, ask the midwife to come right away because you are about to become a father.'"

My grandfather Alessandro Mussolini was born in Montemaggiore, a village in Predappio, on September 11, 1854, to a family of poor farmers. He couldn't attend school and, thus, all his life, felt a little ill at ease with my grandmother Rosa because she had been able to pursue her studies. She was born five years later than him, in Villafranca di Forlì. She was the daughter of a veterinarian, "an empirical veterinarian," as my father would say.

My grandparents Alessandro and Rosa were married in 1882. My father, the first of their three children, was born exactly a year after they were married. "And do you know why" he asked us once, "I was given the name Benito?" We didn't. He explained, "They named me Benito in memory of Benito Juarez, the famous Mexican revolutionary." So, ever since then, the Mussolinis have been breathing the air of revolt and struggle.

Villa Carpena is part of my fondest memories. I now go back there often when I pass through Romagna on my concert tours. Even if it means taking the long way, I am always glad to stop at Forlì and Villa Carpena.

My father joined us for brief periods during the long summer vacations we would spend there with our mother. He arrived alone at the wheel of his Fiat 1500 or accompanied by agent Berardi, who remained at his side for many years. When she would see him appear at the villa gates, my mother would rush to open them with her heart racing. I'm not exaggerating. She wrote this herself in her diary, "My husband's arrival was the most wonderful thing that could happen to me."

He would park the Fiat in the garden, and our magical, golden vacation would begin. Nothing could disturb us. The garden of Villa Carpena seemed like a forest to us. Father would survey the trees planted by my mother and his brother Arnaldo. My uncle Arnaldo was an ecologist, a man ahead of his time who had a sacred respect for nature.

I have kept some images from those long-gone seasons, yellowed photographs that I take out every once in a while and regard with nostalgia. One of my favorites is that of my brother Bruno looking into the photographer's lens while enjoying a picnic with my other brother Vittorio on a meadow near Villa Carpena. A small tablecloth is spread out on the grass between them. On it the lens captures a loaf of bread broken in the middle and, a little farther behind, a bottle of mineral water and a wicker basket. Bruno and Vittorio are dressed in shorts. Vittorio, in an effort to tame his curly hair, is wearing a hair net. Bruno is seven years old and Vittorio is nine. It is the summer of 1925, two years before I was born.

My mother also liked this photograph very much. In those years, she was living in Milan with my three older siblings (my sister Edda, the oldest, was born in 1910), while my father lived almost permanently in Rome.

Mamma had a great virtue—she remained herself despite her husband's political rise, and in the years to follow, she lived modestly, carefully avoiding pageantry and public display. When she truly couldn't avoid it, her embarrassment and tension were evident.

"I am a country woman," she would say. And, at every opportunity she would return to her Romagna, as well as the other places to which she felt connected throughout her long life. I understand her well because I am just like her in that respect—there are landscapes that become a part of us and to which we continually return, drawn by a mysterious force. Why is this so? I think that only those places where we were children have the power to rejuvenate us. In my case, it's as if those hills, those vineyards, those knolls, and those old manors that peek out here and there across the rises and the valleys are saying, "It is here where you began your journey and here where you can regenerate. Any time you want, your life can begin again here."

In 1925, the year of Bruno and Vittorio's picnic, my father was able to take only a short vacation. He joined my mother from August 6 to August 9 in Cattolica where she was staying with the three children. In thinking about this occasion, I envision another photograph that I hold especially dear. Cast against the sunlight of the Adriatic Riviera, my father is wearing a black jacket and a pair of gray cuffed pants in the latest fashion, like those worn by the young Duke of Windsor; black and white shoes; a white shirt, the collar of which is fastened with a pin; and a pearl-gray tie. He has on a gray felt hat, and he's looking off into the distance, his right arm draped around my sister Edda's shoulders. My sister's hair is cut short, like a boy's, and she's wearing a white dress with a low waist and a thin belt. She has on white leather shoes and gray knit socks—the same color as the blouse peeking out from underneath the short sleeves of her dress.

Edda already had a certain influence over my father. She was very intelligent and determined. When she wanted to engage in an argument, she was vigorous. My brothers and I admired her unreservedly. She captivated us, as she did anyone who came into contact with her.

MY SISTER WAS BORN IN FORLÌ, where my parents lived from 1909 to 1912. Their apartment was located in an old palazzo belonging to the counts of Merenda, on a street that bore the same name.

"We were living in two small rooms that faced a courtyard where the sun never shined," my mother told me. "To reach it, you had to climb a very narrow staircase, so narrow that I almost couldn't pass in the last months that I was pregnant with Edda. We had a bed, a table, exactly two chairs, and one small coal stove. We had neither sheets nor cutlery, so we had to borrow them from my mother.

"Despite all that, I have to confess, Romano, this was one of the most beautiful periods of my life. Your father, who ran a weekly socialist newspaper, *La Lotta di Class (The Class Struggle)*, was all mine, as he would never be again. He was earning one hundred and twenty lira a month. He had to give twenty to the party, and our rent was another fifteen. He would give me the rest, and I practically had to do somersaults to try to save anything."

To the end, my father turned his paycheck over to my mother, untouched—he never even opened the envelope. He had no sense of money. He often got the bills mixed up, not to mention the coins. "When he dies, all he'll have in his pocket will be a handkerchief and his glasses," my mother would say. "He's never carried a single lira on him."

The time they spent on Via Merenda was a happy one for my parents. My mother told me that every morning, my father would leave the house early to go to the newsroom and, on the way, would stop in Forlì's main square. There, at the newsstand, he would quickly leaf through the papers, then finally purchase the one that had published the most interesting articles.

For their first child, he absolutely wanted a daughter while my mother would have preferred a boy. At the time, there were no ultrasounds so it wasn't possible to know the gender of the child in advance. All the same, when Mamma entered her sixth month, my father chose a name for his daughter. He had no doubt that his wish would be fulfilled. "It'll be a girl," he said. "And her name will be Edda. I like this name. I found it in a book."

He bought a wooden crib for fifteen lira, asked the salesperson to decorate it with pink ribbon, and carried it home on his back. He insisted too, at all costs, on being present at the birth. But when the moment came, he didn't get to hear Edda's first cry because he had fainted. As my parents were not yet married, his firstborn was entered in the birth registry as the "daughter of Benito Mussolini and Jane Doe."

Photographs

left: Benito Mussolini during a brief vacation at Villa Carpena with his fourth son, Romano. Forli, Italy. July 1929.

above: Benito Mussolini presiding over a ceremony awarding reclaimed farmland to workers in the new agricultural center of the Pontine Marshes. Sabaudia, Italy. September 20, 1934.

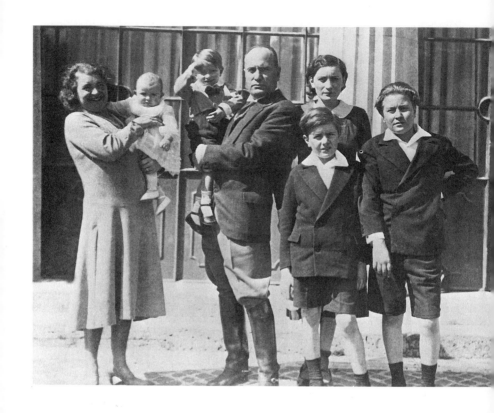

above: Mussolini family portrait. Benito Mussolini with his son Romano in his arms, his wife, Donna Rachele, holding their daughter Anna Maria, and their three other children, Edda, Bruno, and Vittorio. 1932.

right: The Mussolini family during a picnic at Villa Carpena near Forli, Italy. Circa 1934.

above: At the Monaco Conference to discuss the Sudeten mountain range region in Central Europe, from left to right; Galeazzo
Ciano, Benito Mussolini, Adolf Hitler, Edouard Daladier, and
Arthur Neville Chamberlain. Monaco, Germany. September 30,
1938.

following top and bottom: The rescue of Benito Mussolini from
Gran Sasso orchestrated by German troops under the command
of SS Captain Otto Skorzeny. The infamous glider airplane
Fiesler156 C "Stork" took the deposed Il Duce from Gran Sasso
to Pratica di Mare Airport. Campo Imperatore, Italy.
September 12, 1943.

left: Claretta Petacci, Benito Mussolini's mistress. Circa 1940.

above: Benito Mussolini and wife, Donna Rachele. Circa 1940.

above: Ida Dalser with her and Benito Mussolini's illegitimate child Benitio Albino. Circa 1920.

right: Benito Mussolini and wife, Donna Rachele, with their grandchildren at Villa Torlonia, Rome. Circa 1940.

above: Benito Mussolini being honored after having delivered a speech to four thousand Turin officers of the Sub-Alpine division of the Fascist party. Rome. May 30, 1936.

right: A crowd gathers around the display of the bullet-ridden and bludgeoned bodies of Benito Mussolini, his mistress Clareta Petacci, and some of his officers executed at Dongo. The corpses were soon thereafter hung upside down from a gas station railing. Milano, Piazzale Loreto. April 29, 1945.

above: Handwritten inscription on back of the photograph— *Donna Rachele Mussolini, widow of the former Italian dictator, poses with two of her children, Romano and Anna Maria in an Allied detention camp where they are held near Rome. 7-22-45.*

above: Romano Mussolini celebrating the birth of his daughter Alessandra Mussolini with his first wife, Anna Maria Scicolone (right), and her sister, actress Sophia Loren. Rome. January 1963.

following: Romano Mussolini playing the piano. Gargano (Brescia), Italy. October 2002.

CHAPTER 8

Il Duce, the Cinema, and Petrolini

My father had very simple tastes, which my mother knew well and helped to shape with her authentic home cooking. Even when we moved into Villa Torlonia in 1929, she continued to serve simple dishes she prepared herself. She even had some utensils and garden vegetables brought directly from Villa Carpena.

Pastasciutta was Il Duce's favorite first course, followed by a hearty soup, which, unfortunately, gave him heartburn. He also liked boiled chicken quite a bit as well as my mother's pudding and her freshly squeezed grapefruit juice, a rarity in those days. He drank wine only on special occasions. With his meals, which he always consumed in a matter of minutes, he drank sparkling mineral water and would often end with an herbal tea. During business meetings, which frequently ran well into the night, he drank only lemonade and orange juice so as to stay awake and, as he used to say, "avoid the risk of becoming inebriated."

At midday and in the evenings, he liked to have the family around him at Villa Torlonia. He would inquire about our progress in school and, when he didn't like what he heard, Mamma would have to be the mediator. He never raised his voice, but one of his famous stern looks was enough to make us nervous. I must admit, however, that this would seldom occur. In fact, as soon as my father noticed one of us blushing or casting an anxious glance at the others, he changed the subject to relieve the tension.

At our table, no dish could be refused. My mother was unyielding on this matter—everything that was served had to be eaten. At the end of the meal, even pieces of bread would be eaten or saved for the following serving. I remember that once my sister Anna Maria and I complained that we didn't like a certain dish. Nonetheless, our mother asked us to eat it. Then she cautioned us with a phrase in the Romagna dialect, which left a profound impression on us, "Watch out, or I'll send you to eat with Pates!"

In folktales told by the residents of Romagna, Pates was a poor man who depended on the charity of others to satisfy his hunger. To be sent to eat with him, therefore, meant not to eat at all.

Another imaginary creature to which my mother resorted when she wanted to frighten us was the "folletto della stalla," an evil soul who tied animals' tails in knots. Anna Maria and I were deathly afraid of it. I remember as if it were today a time when we were all, for a change, at the table together, and my sister asked my mother, "But doesn't it hurt the animals when the folletto ties their tails?" It was my father who responded, nodding gravely, "It certainly does, the poor things."

AFTER DINNER, IL DUCE generally liked to watch a movie for twenty minutes or so. "It frees my mind," he explained. The ritual had been introduced at Villa Carpena, but it became a real tradition after we moved to Villa Torlonia. The film viewings subsequently took place wherever we lived, from Rocca delle Caminate to Villa Feltrinelli. Here, during the last stage of my father's life and the happiest time for our family, our projectionist was Barilani, a former police officer. Barilani was also Il Duce's trusted personal driver for many years. He was a cordial man, gracious on every occasion when he drove us.

During our stay in Rome, our projectionist was named Guido Baldi, and he too was a likable sort. Sometimes my parents would tell him which film they wanted to see, and other times he would recommend one of the latest releases. He knew their taste. And he knew that my father probably would not see the movie through to its end, while my mother would not go to bed until the last frame read "*Fine.*"

In Rocca delle Caminate, the projectionist would come from Forlì bringing with him the movie we had requested. Charlie Chaplin was my father's favorite actor, and he asked to see *The Gold Rush* and *Modern Times* more than once. He was also amused by the films of Stan Laurel and Oliver Hardy and liked the surreal humor of Harold Lloyd and Buster Keaton.

Obviously, my father was interested in the Italian cinema and considered it an extraordinary means for spreading propaganda. My brother Vittorio, who was a great fan and connoisseur of movies, had many long conversations with my father about directors and actors and kept him abreast of all the important developments.

VITTORIO WAS ONLY TWENTY-ONE IN 1937 when my father sent him on his first trip to Hollywood. There he met Hal Roach, the producer of Laurel and Hardy films, to try to find a way to produce a series of films adapted from grand operas.

In that same year, Vittorio was working for *Cinema* magazine, a biweekly publication on the "seventh art," which served as a touchstone not only for those involved in the film industry, but also for popular culture. So when my brother asked my father if he could use several rooms in Villa Torlonia as an editorial office, permission was granted immediately.

The magazine had illustrious contributors. Between 1937 and 1943, articles were published by Giuseppe Prezzolini, Lucio D'Ambra, Michelangelo Antonioni, Giuseppe Ungaretti, Corrado Alvaro, Luigi Chiarini, Domenico Meccoli, Francesco Pasinetti, Emilio Cecchi, and Goffredo Coppola. Vittorio, who was the magazine's editor in chief, could also count on other high-caliber correspondents such as Frank Capra and Sacha Guitry to send him articles and photographs from around the world.

And what about the Italian cinema? As I said, it was very important to my father. One of his ideas was to encourage its extensive development and transform it into an industry as well organized as Hollywood. Vittorio was his consultant, one might say, and his first big production was the famous film *Luciano Serra, Pilot.*

Senator Giovanni Agnelli, a major stockholder in Fiat, funded the production. It was directed by Goffredo Alessandrini, already known for *Cavalleria.* My brother took on the job of supervising the production. He hired a young man as one of the scriptwriters, who was, as he put it, "always in my way"—Roberto Rossellini. The most popular actor of the time, Amedeo Nazzari, was signed to play the lead role.

My father, despite his countless obligations, followed the production of *Luciano Serra, Pilot* with great interest. The film was an enormous success and was even sold abroad, which was a true rarity in those days.

In 1938, Vittorio visited the Babelsberg Center in Berlin, the German counterpart to Cinecittà which was launched at that time. Hitler himself closely followed the film industry. "But more than anything," my brother later told me, "Hitler was fascinated by the long-distance broadcasting of images. The first television experiments dated back to 1932. But when I visited Babelsberg, the technical capabilities were already very advanced and the Führer had equipment similar to that used in the 1950s for the first public television broadcasts. He was convinced that all communication in the future would take place via television." My father shared this opinion, but in Italy we lagged a bit behind. The first steps toward broadcasting images were not taken until 1934.

At Babelsberg, my brother had long conversations with the heads of two large production houses, UFA

Film and Terra Film. As others did in Hollywood, he made plans in Babelsberg for a series of major co-productions. My father's dream was reflected in Vittorio's dream, but my brother neglected to take into account the war, which would set the world afire only a few months later and halt all international co-productions.

Vittorio's strategy was to cast a wide net. Between 1939 and 1940, he reached an agreement with Jean Renoir, the famous director of *The Grand Illusion*. The director was to move from Paris to Rome and shoot three films for the Scalera production house. The first was to be *Tosca,* an adaptation inspired by Puccini's opera. The second was *Rigoletto*, even though at that point the script was still incomplete. The third was a melodrama, a love story set in the Paludi Pontine marshes.

Renoir was very enthusiastic about the projects. He came to Rome, signed the contract, and set to work. A few days later, the war broke out and, to the French director's and my brother's great disappointment, everything evaporated. "Our collaboration was interrupted," the two said during a modest press conference, "in anticipation of better days."

I would like to add a little-known fact. In 1941, my brother wrote the story for *The Three Pilots*, one of the first films in which Alberto Sordi played the lead. It was directed by Mario Mattioli. Leonardo Cortese and Michela Belmonte, sister of the more famous Maria Denis, had the other two leading roles. Under the pseudonym Tito Silvio Mursino, my brother produced two more films, both directed by Roberto Rossellini: *A Pilot*

Returns, with Massimo Girotti and Michela Belmonte, and *The Man with the Cross*, with Alberto Tavazzi and Roswita Schmidt.

My father also liked music and the theater. The composer Pietro Mascgni, famous throughout Europe for his *Cavalleria Rusticana,* and the conductor Victor de Sabata were both his personal friends. The latter had made numerous appearances in America, and his interpretations of Wagner and Verdi, two of Il Duce's favorite composers, were considered works of genius. I remember that he had several concerts at Villa Torlonia, which, thanks to Edda's and Vittorio's acquaintances, had become a hub for culture and art. My mother used to call Edda "the intellectual of the family."

Everyone is familiar with my father's passion for the violin. My mother told me that in the house on Via Merenda, he would play it over Edda's cradle in order to soothe her. I too enjoyed listening to him play.

Some will be surprised to learn that my father was also a fan of jazz. I was only four years old when I heard this music for the first time. It was in 1931, at Villa Carpena, when my brother Vittorio brought the first 78 rpm records to our house and later introduced me to the majestic interpretations of Duke Ellington and other jazz greats.

I'd like to return now to my father's relationship with the theater. "Ettore Petrolini," he said, "was a genius. His *Nerone,* an original satirical 'pastiche' on dictatorship, was especially entertaining. But who knows why the journalists avoided mentioning that I was seated in the first row of the Valle Theater in Rome when it opened." Petrolini was born in 1886, three years after my father. Il Duce said of him, "he was spirited to the last. He wrote his second autobiography in 1936, the same year he died. And what else could he have named it but *Partly by Choice, Partly to Cheat Death?*"

MY FATHER was extremely skilled at keeping the public Mussolini and the private Mussolini separate—perhaps without wanting to—but he didn't want to involve us in his problems, and he succeeded in this, thanks to a series of elaborate and simple techniques, of which I only much later became aware. He knew, for example, that I liked listening to music on my own. At Villa Torlonia, we had a large phonograph with a horn. To concentrate, I would sink into a big wicker armchair. Well, it was my father himself who arranged to have this phonograph and this armchair follow the family there all the way from Romagna.

His displays of affection were surprising too. At times he seemed to live more for others than for himself. He wanted all of us to be happy, to avoid the trials and tribulations that he had to face—on big or small occasions.

I'll explain what I mean with a concrete example. At Villa Torlonia, my refuge was an attic I would reach by using a small ladder, which I would then pull up after me, thus isolating myself from the world. From this attic—though I would do better to call it a penthouse because it was a sprawling space, as was the rest of the villa placed at my father's disposal by Prince Torlonia for a symbolic rent of one lira per year—my view stretched over a marvelous park.

I would watch Rome at sunset. The sight was captivating and I wished I could make out the fine details that were lost in the immensity of it all. But to do so I would have needed a telescope. And, indeed, without ever having said a word to anyone about it, I found a telescope one day in my hideaway. My father was capable of such sensitivity.

CHAPTER 9

Edda, My Father, and Galeazzo Ciano

Edda, my adored older sister, died on April 8, 1995, fifty years after my father. As one of the disturbing, recurring coincidences in our family's history, she died in what my mother called "our fatal month," April. Just think: my father died on the 28th, my sister Anna Maria on the 25th, and Edda's younger son Marzio on the 11th. My daughter, Alessandra, put it best: we Mussolinis should erase that month from the calendar.

Edda was an unusual woman. Of all the children, she most resembled my father. She had his temperament (energetic to the point of recklessness), his analytical skill, and his raging sensitivity. She resembled him physically too, with that withering look she inherited from him.

I was still a child in the 1930s when she shook Italy with her nonconformist look. Extremely well educated, she spoke English, French, and German as fluently as she did Italian. She drove dangerously and smoked in public, just like the Hollywood divas, but with a sporty elegance. In Rome, everyone competed to join her circle of friends.

My father had a weakness for her, which he made no attempt to conceal. I still remember the tone of his voice when he called us from Greece in March 1943. The war was in full swing, and he was visiting the front lines when someone informed him that the *Po,* a ship on which Edda was serving as a Red Cross nurse, had been torpedoed and bombed.

My mother motioned for me to come closer when she was on the telephone with him. I could hear for myself his concern as he said, "You know, Edda fell into the sea." And then, "Just imagine, she was in the water for five hours but now she's safe. I'll be flying to Albania in a little while. I want to see for myself that she's all right."

The following day we received his long telegram from the General Command in Albania in which he recounted Edda's odyssey. "Seven English bombs hit the *Po* in the middle of the night and it sank quickly. Edda was in her cabin during the attack and was suddenly awakened. Instinctively, she took an overcoat and rushed outside. Reaching the cabin of her friend, who was also a Red Cross nurse and someone with whom she had studied in Milan, she tried in vain to open the door a blast from one of the bombs had blocked, while the poor woman trapped on the other side pleaded for help.

"Edda was trying to save her friend using all of her strength when the ship tilted to one side. A raging river of water flooded the hallway as all the lights went out. Edda was paralyzed with fear. Right at that moment, a sailor grabbed her by the arm and dragged her outside. A few seconds later, she found herself in the water trying to help those around her. She was rescued after five hours, at the first light of dawn."

Edda was saved that time, but a short while later, my

brother Bruno's fate would unfortunately turn out quite differently. Still my memories pull me to my sister's glory years and to that long run during the 1930s when she was admired by all. Even Hitler himself held her in high regard.

For Edda and her husband, Galeazzo, those were unforgettable times. She always liked to travel and had the opportunity to do so. Of the Mussolini women, she appeared in public most often. I fondly remember, for example, when, in 1934, she returned from a long voyage she had taken to China with Galeazzo. That year she had also spent a good deal of time in London, where Dino Grandi was serving as ambassador and had achieved notable personal success.

Edda was truly very popular. My father would always say of her, "She enjoys a distinct state of grace." He wasn't wrong. In September 1934, when Galeazzo was named by my father Undersecretary for Press and Propaganda, the first stage of his political ascent, she became the regime's "First Lady." Within a short time, she also became its most visible mother when little Fabrizio came into the world, and, a few years later, two other children as well—Raimondina, nicknamed "Idina," and Marzio. Becoming a grandfather affected my father deeply. "I feel as if I've gone back in time," he would say to my mother. "I confuse my grandchildren with my children. Whoever thinks that having grandchildren makes you old is wrong. For me, exactly the opposite is true."

At the start of the Ethiopian campaign, when he was appointed minister, Galeazzo was only thirty-two years old. Edda carried on with her official activities, representing the family during her husband's assignment in East Africa. She handed out awards and diplomas and participated in various events. As her circle of admirers grew, everything she did met with approval and was held up as a model for others to follow.

The gossip grew as well. Edda and Galeazzo, the prototype of a modern, nonconformist couple, were said to live separate lives. He, a handsome man who had always been surrounded by women, was said to have continued to have love affairs after their marriage. She, a free spirit and not about to tolerate betrayal, was said to have repaid him in equal measure.

I have to say that I have never seen proof of all these affairs. I am also convinced that the rumors about Edda were unfounded. The truth is that my sister was an affectionate and attentive mother to her children, much more so than could be possible if she were the uninhibited wife she was rumored to be.

One thing is certain: each of her escapades became, as we say today, trendy. Her ideas were contagious, especially for us in the family. For example, when Edda came back from a trip to Brazil with a jaguar, my father kept it for a time at Villa Torlonia. After that, keeping ferocious animals as house pets became quite fashionable in Italy.

In addition to Edda's jaguar, for a while Villa Torlonia was also home to a golden eagle and to Rai and Italia—a pair of lions that later had three cubs. There were also Cocò the monkey, a deer, two gazelles, a falcon, parrots, canaries, Bibì and Bibò the turtles, and two graceful ponies that were gifts for Anna Maria and me.

Edda and Galeazzo's meeting came about because he was the son of Admiral Costanzo Ciano, one of my father's supporters who was very close to him during the crisis following Giacomo Matteotti's assassination. Over time, their friendship came to include the families and, as my mother explains, "was strengthened in 1930 by Edda and Galeazzo's engagement. Your sister was eighteen years old at the time and had been in love previously with the son of a famous industrialist from Romagna, Orsi Mangelli. She met him during a trip to Spain. One evening, having been invited to dinner at our villa in Riccione, he asked your father if he could speak to him in private. Do you know what he wanted to ask? You'll never guess. He asked about Edda's dowry. The response was clear. 'My daughter has nothing, just as I have nothing.' The young Orsi Mangelli never showed his face again."

Edda and Galeazzo's marriage was planned for April 24, 1930. "Villa Torlonia," my mother said, "was transformed into a greenhouse filled with white flowers. I didn't think Edda was old enough to be married, but it's a well known belief that to their parents, children always remain children. Your father, however, was a wreck. 'She's too young, and she could have waited a little longer.' And so, our house became empty before its time."

To say that my mother was excited about Edda's wedding would be a lie. She evidently had a premonition of sorts. Something bothered her.

She remembered the day of Edda's engagement to Galeazzo, half jokingly and half seriously, "I felt I had to list my firstborn daughter's virtues and flaws for my future son-in-law. I explained that she was good and loyal, but also proud and headstrong. I added that she was very intelligent, but that she couldn't boil an egg, not to mention iron. 'Don't say,' I concluded, 'that I didn't warn you.'"

The wedding ceremony was held in our church, St. Giuseppe on Via Nomentana in Rome, and was attended by four hundred people. The Prince of Torlonia and Dino Grandi were Edda's witnesses. In a twist of fate, it was also Grandi, thirteen years later, who presented the Grand Council with the motion to remove my father from office—Galeazzo signed the motion and thus was later condemned to death as a Grand Council conspirator for having committed high treason against Il Duce.

Following the ceremony and the reception, the newlyweds left for their honeymoon in Capri. My father, who seemed not to want to part with Edda, accompanied them as far as Rocca di Papa. My mother said, "Il Duce cried when he said good-bye because the thought of losing his firstborn daughter terrified him. They fought often because they had such similar and pugnacious natures, so much so that he once said: 'I've managed to bend Italy, but I doubt I will ever be able to bend Edda's will.' Yet he truly adored her.

"I remember our return from Rocca di Papa where we finally left them to continue alone to Capri." My father and mother slowly took their seats in the car that was to return them to Villa Torlonia. They sat in the back. It was a very sad trip. For the first few kilometers, they rode in silence. Then my father said, "Let's hope that Galeazzo can make our daughter happy."

Soon after the wedding, Galeazzo was appointed consul to Shanghai, and, much to my father's regret, he and Edda left for China. But my father was thrilled when Guglielmo Marconi enabled him to speak with her—for my father, Marconi's invention of radio communications erased the distance between Rome and Shanghai.

Edda eventually grew terribly unhappy. I remember her despair on January 8, 1944, when the trial against the Grand Council conspirators, the ones who earlier gave a no-confidence vote in Il Duce, began in the Castelvecchio in Verona. It was a hearing with a foregone conclusion. Hitler himself insisted that the traitors be punished without pity and without exception. Il Duce, having attempted in vain to defend Galeazzo, who was both his former minister of foreign affairs and his daughter's husband, was forced to acquiesce despite the fact that Edda tried to the last to save him.

After arguing violently with my father, and as part of her efforts to save her husband, my sister tried to use Galeazzo's controversial diaries, hidden in a secure location, as currency. She knew that the Germans wanted them and she even requested an audience with Hitler about them. But it was all for naught. On October 19, 1943, Galeazzo, who had sought refuge in Germany on Edda's advice, was forced to board a plane and go back to Verona where he was immediately arrested.

Poor Galeazzo. His fate was sealed. Hitler even held his and my sister's three children hostage in Germany, fearing that Il Duce would find a last-minute escape route for his son-in-law.

On January 10, 1944, at two o'clock in the afternoon, the verdict was delivered—death for everyone except Cianetti, who was given thirty years. That same night, Alessandro Pavolini planned to deliver to my father a plea for clemency but then changed his mind. "I spared Il Duce from having to confirm my sentence," he later explained.

Galeazzo was executed as a traitor the next morning, January 11. When my father learned of it, he feigned indifference, but I remember how he burst into tears that evening at Villa Feltrinelli. He cried without attempting to hide his pain. That he had no news from Edda tore him up even further.

That night was long and terrible for all of us. My mother held my sister Anna Maria and me by the hand, not daring to knock on my father's door. Our family tragedy took place within the larger tragedy of Italy, like a wave of intolerable grief.

False are the accounts that Galeazzo's execution produced a rift between Edda and all the other members of the Mussolini family. It is false that from that moment forward she hated us with all her might. In fact, after the end of the war, having just been liberated from her confinement at Lipari, my sister immediately joined my mother, my sister Anna Maria, and me in Ischia, where we were being detained. Edda then rented her own house nearby to stay close to us.

Edda needed to take her mind off of things, to stop herself from constantly thinking about what had happened. She later turned to me for help of sorts. I remember in the 1950s and 1960s when, united by a passion to win the lottery, we formed a small pool to play. If we were apart, we would consult each other by telephone. When we saw each other, we would make plans for spending the big winnings—which never came.

I remember Edda with immense and profound affection. The thing that most often comes to mind about her, and that fills me with tenderness each time I recall it, is the readiness with which she welcomed into her home Marina, my brother Bruno's orphaned daughter. Our brother died in a famous air crash in 1941. Later, in 1946, his wife Gina drowned in Lake Como. Edda always treated Marina like her own daughter. Marina stayed with her until the day she got married. To me these are in no way the actions of a woman who profoundly hated the members of her own family.

CHAPTER 10

Assassination Season

The first attempt on my father's life was uncovered and thwarted on November 4, 1925. There has been a great deal written about this subject, and the OVRA (Organizzazione di Vigilanza Repressione dell'Antifascismo) was often said to be directly implicated in organizing the attempt in order to provide the regime with an excuse for striking back at its enemies. Nothing could be further from the truth, and I believe I can confirm in all honesty, nothing could be more historically incorrect. Besides, the secret police weren't equipped to prevent assassinations and conspiracies, let alone stage false ones.

In our house, we breathed easily, which, even now, after so many years' distance still seems surprising. My father gave no hint whatsoever of what would have been legitimate fears—in fact, security measures were reduced to a minimum. In reality, he was one step away from death on more than one occasion, and he only escaped thanks to a series of circumstances that share an element of the surreal.

My mother was the only one who had a true grasp of the situation, which, only miraculously, did not end in tragedy. But how could she induce a man who refused all caution to be more prudent? "Everything happening around me," my father used to say, "leaves me indifferent. I consciously choose 'Live dangerously' as my life's motto. As an old soldier, I say, 'If I advance, follow me. If I retreat, kill me. If they kill me, vindicate me.'"

The conspiracy planned for November 4, 1925, implicated the very well known socialist politician Tito Zaniboni; the commander of the Second Army in the First World War General Luigi Capello; the journalist Giuseppe Donati; the representative of the Partito Popolare Carlo Quaglia; and another journalist by the name of Grimaldi.

Il Duce was to be killed while addressing a group of war veterans on National Unity Day from a balcony at the Palazzo Chigi. The conspirators' plan was for Tito Zaniboni to shoot from a height above my father—from a room in the Hotel Dragoni, to be exact—using a precision rifle.

Everything was planned down to the smallest detail. Two hours before the scheduled assassination, at eleven o'clock in the morning, the rifle was already mounted on a tripod in the hotel room and aimed at the curtains drawn across the Palazzo Chigi balcony. The person responsible for executing this piece of the plan was never discovered. One thing is certain, however—it wasn't Tito Zaniboni, who had done everything in his power to be noticed in his Alpine division major's uniform while he waited among the veterans to hear Il Duce's speech. Zaniboni's plan was then to leave the crowd at an opportune moment and make his way unnoticed to the hotel room. From there, with my father a clear target and the rifle already in place, he was to have opened fire.

It was only a few minutes before eleven when one of the conspirators, Carlo Quaglia, notified the police. He later explained that he feared the consequences of the assassination. Zaniboni was arrested before he was able to reach the room in the Hotel Dragoni, just as my father was stepping out onto the Palazzo Chigi balcony. A few hours later, in Torino, General Capello was also arrested.

At this point, my reasons for insisting on the falsehood of any claims that the assassination was organized by the secret police must be clear to everyone.

The assassination attempt had an enormous effect on the whole country. Zaniboni and Capello were tried and condemned to thirty years in prison, while their accomplices received lesser sentences.

And what about my father? Whenever our family spoke of this event, my brother Vittorio would remember my father's stoic composure. The day after the failed assassination attempt, Il Duce stepped out onto the Palazzo Chigi balcony again to address the crowd gathered in expectation of his appearance. Il Duce said, among other things, "People of Rome, I thank you from the bottom of my heart for this enthusiastic and brotherly show of support. You know that if I had been shot while standing at this railing, they would not have struck a tyrant, but a servant of the Italian people. The government has taken and will take all necessary measures to convince enemies of the regime that there is nothing left they can do. But I demand, I say demand, that there be no senseless civil unrest and no sporadic or individual outbreaks of violence."

ANOTHER ASSASSINATION ATTEMPT was made on April 7, 1926, when a fifty-year-old Irish woman, Violet Albina Gibson, approached my father on the Piazza del Campidoglio in Rome. Moments before, Il Duce had officially opened the Seventh International Surgical Convention in the Orazi and Curiazi Hall, and at that point was encircled by the authorities before coming out to wave to the crowd.

Petite and nervous, Gibson, clutching a pistol, made her way to the front of the crowd. She fired twice, aiming for Il Duce's head. One bullet missed entirely, the other grazed my father's nose.

Even though Il Duce's face was covered with blood, he immediately realized that he had not been critically injured. He then approached the captured would-be assassin and laughed mockingly at her poor aim. He recounted, "Just a few steps away from me were dozens of famous surgeons, all intent on coming to my aid. At that moment, I was frightened indeed!" He later told me jokingly, "That day I truly stared death in the face, but I tell you, I was more afraid of the doctors than of Violet Gibson."

Violet Gibson was taken into custody, where she was interrogated with the help of an interpreter. A few days later, my father ordered her release, convinced that she was mentally imbalanced. The English government, who had already relayed its apologies via its ambassador, officially thanked him.

"ON SEPTEMBER 11, 1926," my mother told me, "there was another attempt on your father's life. His car was crossing the Piazzale di Porta Pia in Rome when a young man threw a hand grenade. Four passersby were seriously wounded in the explosion, but Il Duce, unscathed, proceeded to Palazzo Chigi as if nothing had happened. The assassin made no attempt to flee. His name was Gino Luccetti; he was twenty-one years old and an anarchist. He had secretly come from France where he was known by the nom de guèrre Ermete Giovannini."

A little more than a month passed. Then, on October 31, 1926, my father's life was again saved by a miracle. This assassination attempt took place in Bologna, where Il Duce had arrived the previous day to dedicate a new sports stadium. This building was among Europe's most beautiful.

Here is the scene: After delivering the opening speech for the Fifteenth Conference of the Italian Society for Scientific Advancement at the Archiginnasio Library, my father was heading toward the station in an open car. Because of the crowd, the car was forced to slow down. All of a sudden, from somewhere in the crowd, two shots were fired. One bullet completely missed its target, while the other grazed the medals on my father's honorary police lance corporal's uniform.

As the car accelerated to protect my father from any further attempts on his life, a well-known Bolognese fascist, Arconovaldo Bonaccorsi, thought he identified the assassin as a fourteen-year-old boy, Anteo Zamboni, wearing dark colors and a black shirt. He gave the boy a terrible blow to the head, and the boy fell to the ground where he was furiously attacked by an angry mob. His autopsy revealed fifteen stab wounds, two gunshot wounds, and multiple fractures.

My father never forgot Anteo Zamboni's death. In September of 1928, when a special tribunal prepared its case for the Bologna assassination attempt, the boy's deposition posed serious problems for the judges. Il Duce declared that he had, in fact, seen the shooter and that it was a man dressed in light colors with a hat on his head, not Anteo Zamboni, who had been dressed in dark colors and wore no hat. What's more, according to my father, the shots were fired from the opposite side of where the boy had been standing.

AFTER THESE ASSASSINATION ATTEMPTS, the only safety measure Il Duce agreed to was to permit two escort cars to follow his. My mother told us that his guardian angels were always by his side from the moment he drove away, quite cheerfully. "When he leaves Rome," she would say, "your father always has someone to see or some ceremony to attend. For security reasons, sometimes his destinations would be kept from the public. But as soon as word got out that he had arrived in a place, a sea of people would gather around. Escorts and guardian angels, indeed! Really, anyone could approach him and make an attempt on his life."

My mother said that I was frightened by the throngs of people that would gather around my father. It's true,

I was. Even today, I have a sense of uneasiness when I drive down a dug-up street and see the dust rise behind me. It immediately brings to mind the dust clouds that announced Papà's arrival in one of his sports cars to those of us waiting for him at Villa Carpena. He was always in danger, despite his confident demeanor.

How many times I had heard assassinations discussed in the family! "They became so frequent," my mother wrote, "that this word began to sound common, even to the children. This was especially true for Romano, who was born in 1927 shortly after some of the most publicized attempts." Still, it wasn't easy getting used to the idea that, at any moment, someone could bring death to our family. A quiet agony was present at all times, affecting the way we acted.

Still, in my mother's words, "I remember when Romano threw a series of tantrums at Villa Torlonia because his father wanted to send him to bed (it was already after ten o'clock in the evening). On this particular occasion, we were watching a western in our screening room and Romano wanted to stay up to see the end. But Il Duce remained firm. Romano left, and after a little while, I sent his brother Bruno to see whether he had gone to sleep."

My mother was right to worry. Instead of going to my bedroom, I had climbed up to the loft overhanging the sitting room where our screenings were held. When Bruno tracked me down, he found me in the darkest corner with a small wooden gun in my hand. "What are you doing?" he asked. And I responded, quite seriously, "I want to assassinate Papà."

In sum, assassination was a genuine obsession for our family, even if our fears, curiously, never resulted in any specific precautionary measures. Neither my mother nor my sister Edda ever had security guards, nor did my brothers Vittorio and Bruno, even though they wore military uniforms beginning at a young age. As for me, it seems to have never occurred to anyone that I could have been kidnapped or in any way placed in danger.

CHAPTER 11

My Mother's Rivals

I've already talked about my mother's encounter with Claretta Petacci and the following desperate act of drinking bleach. When the doctor declared that my mother was out of danger after her attempted suicide, my father sat next to her bed and took her hand. They remained like this for a long while, not moving, exchanging only a few words from time to time. I watched them through the half-closed door, a thousand thoughts running through my head. I felt like I was watching a movie or, better yet, the epilogue of a movie that brings everyone back to reality after long sequences marked by confusion and fantasy. Like so many others, and perhaps more so than others, I felt that we Mussolinis were a family at the mercy of the winds in a wretched Italy overwhelmed by war.

The sense of security that our father had given us, plus all of the traditional common sense that was the cornerstone of my mother's presence, indeed, all of our hopes of surviving the war intact, were at that moment lost to me. Everything vanished in an instant before my bewildered eyes. The only reality remaining for me seemed to be that this couple, no longer young, was so cruelly being put to a test. Did this couple—doubled up with pain, holding each other's hands—ever really love each other? Or was their life together a frantic race during which they had simply avoided looking each other in the eye?

ALL OF THE RUMORS I had heard about my father's lovers came to my mind then. I remembered the embarrassed silence of us children and my mother's tears—tears I only came to understand just a few years ago ....

Il Duce and Angelica Blabanoff, the famous militant socialist in the editorial office of Il Popolo d'Italia, had a notorious relationship. There were those who even claimed she was Edda's mother! And my mother was humiliated, not reacting, pretending not to know and not to hear, not only on this occasion, but later as well, many years later, when I had become her confidant and she related her difficult history as a wife.

Il Duce's relationship with Margherita Sarfatti also hurt my mother. A fascinating intellectual Jewish woman, she had a tremendous influence on my father. She dedicated a book to him, Dux (it was even reprinted recently), in which she skillfully paints a portrait of his ascent to power. My father wrote the preface for this work and my mother felt more marginalized and distressed at that moment than perhaps ever before.

"Of all of your father's women," she once told me, "I was jealous only of those who had a place in his mind. The rest didn't interest me."

A wise woman, my mother. My father's exuberance, which she came to know well from the moment he entered her life when he was little more than a boy, didn't trouble her. She knew that there were men in this world who were incapable of controlling their drives and men who were more restrained. At times it's only a matter of hormones. But when to this you add intellectual drive, in which my father certainly wasn't lacking, self-control became impossible. It's remarkable that women, almost all women, are attracted to such men when in reality, they should be wary of them.

Entire books have been written about my father's romantic exploits. My brother Vittorio used to say that many of these accounts were exaggerated. "If Papà really had all of the affairs that are attributed to him," he argued, "he would not have become Il Duce."

Vittorio was right, but I was always struck by my father's truly magnetic appeal. I remember our summers in Riccione when I was about ten years old and he would come to visit us. Sometimes piloting the hydroplane himself, he would descend on a strip of sea not far from our house. A motorboat would then meet him and bring him to the beach. There, all of a sudden, he would find himself surrounded by dozens of screaming girls and women—the "ondine," as my mother used to call them sarcastically. Their eyes shined with the same light.

Men will understand what I'm talking about; women, too. For many years, wherever he went, my father would find himself encircled by "ondine."

They were simple girls and intellectual women, actresses and princesses. While on the subject of princesses, it's not happenstance that at a certain point Maria José was said to be involved with Il Duce. I don't know the details of this episode, and I even tend to believe that there was no emotional tie between my father and the then Princess of Piemonte, but it is likely that even she felt flattered by the rumors that my father admired her.

There is one name on the long list of my father's female conquests that I have, up until now, mentioned only in passing. It is that of Ida Dalser, the young thirty-year-old who for years introduced herself as Mrs. Mussolini, claiming rightly so, I learned only as an adult, to having given my father a son, Benito Albino.

Dalser, the first of four children born to the mayor of Sopramonte in the province of Trento, met my father in her hometown in 1909 after he had been named director of the Labor Department of Austria's Socialist Party. They saw each other again four years later in Milano, where he ran the socialist newspaper Avanti! However, he was no longer unattached as he had already become Edda's father, but neither was he married, since he and my mother were not wed until December 16, 1915, in a civil ceremony, and ten years later, in 1925, in a religious ceremony.

A child was born from my father's affair with Dalser, and he was entered into the birth registry on November 11, 1915, as Benito Dalser. Two years later, my father recognized the child as his, and before the notary public Buffoli in Monza, he agreed to pay 200 lira a month for child support.

At this point, instead of pulling back as my father had hoped, Dalser began continually showing up to see him, and he no longer knew how to free himself from her. My mother reluctantly remembered these events, as I still do. Nevertheless, I thought it appropriate to give Dalser her place here. When all is said and done, she gave my father a son, and, from that moment on, her life certainly could not have been easy.

The meeting between my mother and Dalser took place in 1917. Having been called up for service in the war, my father was wounded by a grenade launcher in Carso and was sent to recover in a military hospital in Milan. Both my mother and Ida Dalser visited him there, each arriving without the other's knowledge until suddenly they found themselves face-to-face.

"At that moment," my mother told me, "I didn't recognize her. It was she who recognized me. She threw herself at me in your father's room, insulting me and screaming, 'I am Mussolini's wife! Only I have the right to be at his side!' The soldiers there started to laugh. Wild with anger, I lunged at her and grabbed her by the neck. From his bed, looking like a mummy with bandages restraining his movement, Benito attempted to intervene. He got up from his bed to stop us while a doctor and two nurses also tried their best to separate us. Dalser fell back, and I burst into tears."

The relationship with Ida Dalser had long-standing repercussions and preoccupied my father for years. Even at the height of the Fascist regime, this woman continued to declare herself Mussolini's real wife, presenting their son Benito Albino as proof.

Through the end of 1922, the year of the March on Rome, her continued appearances were a nightmare for my father. I never spoke to him about it, but I know that he wasn't insensitive to her suffering, especially since the poor woman, who simply couldn't resign herself to staying away from him, eventually grew extremely depressed and irrational.

It's understandable that when people cannot control themselves, they are viewed with suspicion, even if they happen to be telling the truth. If their provocations continue, they manage to antagonize even those who initially supported them. In short, showing signs of mental imbalance leads to trouble as friends begin to distance themselves. Imagine Ida Dalser's isolation as my father began to achieve absolute power and the number of his loyal supporters as well as sycophants multiplied.

Dalser repeatedly crashed into the barrier that kept her from reaching Il Duce until she finally gave up. She fell gravely ill and began to go in and out of hospitals. Benito Albino also fell ill. She died in 1937, he in 1942.

.... Life can be very cruel. This is what I was thinking as I watched my parents through the half-closed door. And the more I watched them, the more I became convinced that despite everything, they were profoundly connected. They had gone through so much together, from their early struggles to the golden years when all of Italy hung on every word from Il Duce's lips. They found themselves together in the middle of a war that no one wanted and whose catastrophic developments no one expected. Now, side by side once again, they had reached their last resort, and not just metaphorically. The small resort town of Gargnano was wrapped inside my father's last, impossible, but cherished dream of marital recovery.

FOLLOWING THE MEETING WITH CLARETTA PETACCI, my mother left the "house of the dead," broken in spirit. It was raining and it had become dark; the meeting had lasted three hours in all. My father's loyal supporter at that time but later his betrayer, Buffarini Guidi, took his place in the car beside her and, along with the chauffeur Nino Martini, headed for Villa Feltrinelli.

During the short ride, my mother didn't say a single word to Buffarini. Even he had convinced her, always pretending not to know about Petacci. She had trusted him, but that afternoon his demeanor revealed not only that Il Duce had often seen his lover, but that he had seen her regularly, right from the beginning.

My mother couldn't contain herself any longer and burst into uncontrollable crying. When they finally arrived at Villa Feltrinelli, the loyal chauffeur Martini and a young German captain who was Il Duce's orderly and also a man very fond of my mother, tried to console her. Their efforts were futile because, as you now know, a short while later my mother would attempt the desperate suicidal act of drinking bleach.

"YOU DIDN'T HEAR what your father and I confided to each other," my mother later said to me. "Little by little, I recovered from the terrible period I had been through. After all, I thought, my husband is still close to me, I haven't lost him. I explained how much I had suffered during the meeting with Petacci. I also told him what I had recently heard—that her brother Marcello Petacci had purchased a large motorboat on the other side of Lago di Garda and intended to use it to kidnap Il Duce. And at this point, I felt overwhelmed again. This woman's shadow haunted me. I was afraid I could no longer cope."

My mother saw some things clearly. Her husband loved her, he was sorry to have made her suffer, and he was wild with pain at the thought of losing her. Despite all of this, however, there was another truth that my mother instinctively avoided—my father was incapable of renouncing Claretta Petacci.

My mother also said this to me, "Everything was sinking and it was too late to separate. All around us, one day after the next, the resentment grew. But meanwhile, the list of the war dead kept growing longer—cousins, nieces and nephews, in-laws, and friends. We were already resigned to the war being lost. Only you and your sister Anna Maria could still be fooled."

It's true. My sister and I wouldn't give up hope. The

trust we had in our father's resourcefulness was stronger than any of our doubts. On July 20, 1944, Il Duce met Hitler in Germany and, upon his return, told us about the secret factories producing "flying bombs," the famous V1 and V2 rockets that everyone had been talking about for years. He himself had seen the deadly arsenals and had no doubt that once they were put into use, the enemy would have no recourse but to surrender.

The V1 and V2 rockets were Anna Maria's and my favorite subject. In her wisdom, our mother shuddered. Il Duce, however, truly believed in our German ally's capacity to recover, or at least he forced himself to believe it.

CHAPTER 12

Bruno's Death Shatters My Father

I was fourteen years old in 1941 when Bruno returned from the Greek campaign. He was to be stationed in Pisa with the four-engine long-range bomber group. Before beginning training on the new aircraft, however, he was sent to Germany for a month, where Hitler, in preparation for a war with the enemy across the Atlantic, was building a series of airports from which the large bombers were to take off.

My father had an affinity for Bruno, a special fondness that almost seemed to be inspired by a sad premonition of the irreversible events that were going to take place. I remember when Bruno returned from Germany. Il Duce asked him to report on the true capabilities of the German air force. Evidently, my father distrusted the information he was receiving from party leaders. Bruno was very clear—his analysis was that despite the Germans' admirable and widespread efforts, they would lose the war. The defeat would represent the fatal epilogue to a conflict that had set them against the entire world. As for Italy, she would be drawn into Germany's crushing defeat.

Bruno confided his worries to my mother as well. "Papà's job is difficult," he said, "but what is most dangerous is all of the sabotage. There are oil tankers that reach their destination safely, only to be inexplicably blown up moments after they arrive. There are weapons that leave the factories with unbelievable flaws. These are not isolated cases, and they are not accidental. These are acts of widespread sabotage that, in a test of truth, will prove to be absolutely disastrous."

My brother had excelled at his career in the Arma Azzura. In 1936, at the age of eighteen, he had already earned a silver medal for valor in the Ethiopian campaign.

In 1937, together with Lieutenant Colonel Attilio Biseo, he set a series of impressive aerial records, risking his life during the Istres-Damascus-Paris air race. The event occurred following a refueling in Damascus, where his S79 took third position. En route to Paris, Bruno and Biseo ran into a violent storm that reached its peak as they were flying over the Alps. I'll quote my brother's account: "All of a sudden, the flight instruments showed a simultaneous loss of power in three of the S79's engines. Biseo and I decided not to waste any time, setting course instead for the small airport in Cameri where we made an emergency landing."

My father, who often proudly spoke of his beloved but unfortunate son's adventures, told me the rest of the story: "The weather was improving, so Bruno was able to set off again for Paris to complete the race at Le Bourget Airport. A few days later, he returned to Italy where I greeted him officially at Littorio Airport." My brother was exultant, my father, even more so.

In 1937, Bruno, again with Biseo, broke the 1,000-kilometer record with a two-ton load by exceeding a speed of 430 kilometers per hour. This is how the famous "Sorci Verdi" squadron was born, with Biseo and several other pilots as members. My father amusingly explained the origin of the squadron name: "While waiting with Bruno for the new S79s to be equipped, Biseo addressed the skeptics, who expected little from these aircraft, and said defiantly, 'Go ahead and turn up your noses. When the S79s begin to fly, we'll give you a hell of a rough time. *Vi faremo vedere i sorci verdi!*'"

When the civil war ended in Spain in March of 1939 with the return of the republicans and Generalissimo Franco's entry into Madrid, my brother didn't hesitate to lend his support. He set off for Palma di Majorca with a bomber squadron. Franco greatly appreciated the gesture, but he also made it known to my father that he had a genuine concern for what could have happened to Bruno had he fallen into enemy hands.

My brother fought in Spain on Franco's behalf for a month and a half, earning, among other things, another silver medal for valor. The news we received about his accomplishments was often confusing. At a certain point, an English newspaper even published an article stating that he was dead.

My mother was constantly afraid. I still remember her heated telephone calls with my father when she learned that Bruno had engaged in a duel with an American pilot, Derek Dickinson, commander of the Red Wings formation. In siding against Franco, the United States had sent the formation in support of the Spanish government.

Bruno broadcast a challenge over the radio, inviting enemy pilots to measure their strength against him—in Spain at that time, in addition to Italians and Germans, there were French, English, and American pilots. Dickinson, who had been stationed in Castellón de la Plana with his squadron, accepted the challenge, saying, "We'll see which of us has tougher skin."

My father was proud of Bruno's courage, but feared for his life. My mother, as I said, was terrified and furious. She argued with Il Duce for allowing his not yet twenty-year-old son to leave for Spain.

Bruno took off from the airport in Palma di Majorca in a Fiat-Romeo, a plane used in military exercises and equipped with only two machine guns. He had a lot of faith in the aircraft because it was extremely easy to handle and was able to make very sharp turns. Derek Dickinson was flying a Boeing P26, possibly the most efficient fighter plane of the time, armed with four machine guns. He left from Castellón de la Plana and headed for Majorca knowing that midway he would encounter Bruno's Fiat-Romeo.

With everything that happens in wars today, it's difficult to believe how the duel between Bruno and Dickinson, indomitable but respected adversaries, much like the knights of days past, actually took place. The duel was to occur at an altitude of 1,000 meters. Flying behind each of the two men were two reconnaissance planes, with their seconds in command on board.

This is how my brother later described the skirmish to the family: "Almost without realizing it, after the umpteenth turn, I found myself above Dickinson's

Boeing. Through the transparent cockpit I saw his silhouette as he was desperately trying to regain altitude. I began to fire my machine guns and I clearly saw my shots hitting the mark. Only later did I learn that Dickinson was wounded in one hand, which prevented him from taking off his scarf and waving it outside to signal surrender, as the terms of our duel required."

Imagine the emotion with which I, a young boy of ten, listened to Bruno's story. I begged him to continue, and he complied—putting an arm around my shoulder and almost whispering into my ear as he began to reconstruct the duel's final moments. "Dickinson's plane took a nosedive for about 400 meters, apparently because Dickinson was dazed by the intense pain in his hand. Then, in an extraordinary effort, he managed to bring the Boeing back up to cruising altitude and I suddenly found him above me. I clearly saw that he had me squarely in his sights but he didn't have time to squeeze the trigger because at that very moment, I raised my right hand and my long scarf in white silk fluttered outside the plane, signaling surrender."

Bruno spoke modestly about the "surrender." In reality, the plane's engine was malfunctioning, leaving him unable to maneuver and forcing him to cut the duel short.

No one has ever published a complete chronicle of this encounter, which, without a doubt, represented one of the "most colorful"—as Bruno used to call it, refusing to use my father's word "memorable"—episodes of the entire Spanish Civil War. If it is in fact true that my brother was forced to cede victory because his engine left him in the lurch, he succeeded in landing unharmed only because of a masterful glide on his part.

Dickinson's Boeing P26 was riddled with 326 hits and his hand was wounded. The American pilot spoke about the duel in a series of interviews to journalists from around the world. The Spanish Civil War was followed with intense interest by the press. Dickinson, assaulted by reporters, embellished his account with ever more astonishing details each time he told it, to the point where he even succeeded in amusing my father. It was Il Duce who sent a clipping of one of these interviews to Bruno in Spain, together with this note: "Here's yet another reconstruction of your famous duel with Captain Dickinson."

Only a few months passed, and Bruno, back from Spain, was already embarking on a new adventure—the first transatlantic flight from Guidonia to Rio de Janeiro aboard three S79s, manufactured by Savoia-Marchetti, from the Sorci Verdi squadron. The first of these planes would be under his command, the second was to be piloted by Biseo, and the third by a Major Moscatelli.

Before the Sorci Verdi left on their new mission, my mother said, as she always did when Bruno took off on one of his exploits, "Please, go slowly." And I can still hear the amused tone and see the affectionate smile with which my brother responded, "Of course, Mamma, you know I will. I have snails in my engines."

My mother told me, "If he could have, Bruno would have said the same thing at the end of July 1941 when he flew to Riccione and dropped to a low altitude twice in order for us to be able to see him."

I too remember seeing Bruno's large aircraft only a few hundred meters above our heads when Edda, Vittorio, and I were vacationing on the Romagna coast. My brother had told us that with the new planes he was testing, he could fly to America and back without stopping. However, in order to succeed, he would have had to abbreviate the Atlantic crossing by leaving from a base in Iceland. "The reality of all this," he would say proudly, "is that with Italian engines, we can achieve extraordinary things. We're number one in the world."

Bruno was right about the efficiency of the planes he was testing. However, he was also perfectly aware that when it came time to face the harsh reality of war, our air force could not be counted on. Apart from the ever more frequent cases of sabotage, especially following the Spanish campaign, the Arma Azzura was showing signs of deep division and was in serious need of complete reorganization.

The reports Il Duce received talked about "flawless aeronautical equipment fully prepared to meet future challenges." In reality, the Spanish exploits had drained Italy's arsenal, which had already been greatly reduced during the Ethiopian War. And while our aircraft scored a series of resounding victories in the Iberian skies, these planes had also suffered the harshest trials during the final year of that war when they faced the fighter planes sent by the Soviet Union in support of the Spanish government. Bruno knew that at any moment, we would be involved in the most difficult and brutal war in history. He knew too that this called for rebuilding the Arma Azzura and equipping it with adequate reserves.

THE LAST TIME I SAW BRUNO was in Riccione in the final days of July 1941. I remember my brother Vittorio and I having so much fun with him. Vittorio was eleven years older than me and he rarely honored us with his company—after taking off his military uniform he became absorbed with his cinema-related pursuits. On this occasion, however, we played ball together and roller-skated along the promenade. Bruno, I remember, slipped and grazed his knee.

On August 7, 1941, at 8:50 in the morning, Bruno took off from the airport in Pisa in the same four-engine plane he had been flying over Riccione a week earlier and in which he wanted to perform a series of specific flight tests. The large plane labored to lift off the runway and managed to do so only at the last moment, after hitting a small cottage with one of its wings. It then pitched up and overturned on Bruno's side. Bruno wasn't wearing a protective helmet, and this is probably why he died. The pilot seated next to him, who was wearing a helmet, survived the crash. Four aviators lost their lives in this air disaster along with Bruno. Vittorio was also supposed to be on that airplane, but he had been called to Rome at the last minute and had decided against joining the flight.

At this point, there is a kind of emptiness in my mind, and my memories get misty, as did my mother's and father's. It was as if all three of us were trying to erase what happened. My mother's account of the terrible hours following Bruno's death, some of which I spent with her, is especially poignant.

"As soon as we received the terrible news," she said, "your father and I boarded a plane for Pisa. I remember that flight. We were thrashed by a violent storm, as if it were a nightmare. The survivors told us that the engines had failed abruptly and that Bruno had done everything possible to avoid a crash. They also told us that he had remained composed to the very end, not giving in to panic. His final words were, 'The battlefield, Babbo!' Someone suggested the possibility of sabotage, and there was an inquiry into that."

I must confess that even I have at times doubted that Bruno's death was an accident, because there were more and more traitors within the regime. Still, no proof has ever been found of tampering on his four-engine plane.

I will always remember how emotional people were when paying their last respects to Bruno, first in Pisa, then in Florence, in Forlì, and finally in Predappio. His remains were buried in the small cemetery in San Cassiano, in a stone tomb bearing only his dates of birth and death. There Bruno rests. A votive lamp burns on his tomb, placed there by the mothers of the airmen of Lucca. I remember that even the English RAF officers who took part in the farewell ceremony paid homage to my brother by sending flowers.

Remembering that unhappy 7th of August, my mother would say, "What hit me hardest was Il Duce's excruciating silence. It was as if he had turned to stone."

I witnessed firsthand my parents' despair, especially my mother's. After the funeral in San Cassiano, she returned to Rocca delle Caminate exhausted and threw herself on the bed in search of relief. She fell asleep almost instantly. Shortly thereafter, she awoke with a cry and rushed into my room, seeking comfort in my arms.

I still shudder at the memory of her words and the events that followed. My mother said she was about to fall asleep when, in a state of semiconsciousness, she sensed Bruno's presence. "Yes, it really was him. He approached and, just as he had done as a child, jumped under the covers and drew close to me. I had so many things I wanted to say to him, but I couldn't speak. Then he said, 'Mamma, I'm cold, warm me up.' Distraught, I caressed his freezing forehead and hands, but then he said, 'Now we must leave each other.'"

My mother, as I said, jumped screaming out of bed and ran into my room. She stayed there, holding me, until she was able to catch her breath again. Later, taking me by the hand, she led me to a room upstairs where she had put away my brother's peaked hat, his shirt, and his blood-soaked vest. She opened the small armoire, took them out, and started to scream, "They're here, right where I put them! So, it's true that my Bruno is dead! And when he came into my bed it was only a dream!"

That night she cried violently as the stormy winds slammed the shutters in Rocca. My mother later told me, "From that moment on, I've had a fear of storms, a fear that I cannot conquer. And also from that moment on, after Bruno's death, I have only sad memories."

My brother's loss also profoundly affected my father and caused a kind of fracture in his life. I remember my brother Vittorio's words, "There was a Mussolini *before* Bruno's death, and a Mussolini *after* it. I'm not saying that prior to August 7, 1941, our father smiled often, but despair was not a part of his emotional range. The tragedy turned him into a different man whose lost stare, at times, provoked pity."

My mother added, "More and more often, your father, a man who could not allow himself to give in to sadness and had to keep his wits about him in order to meet his weighty obligations, had a face marked by suffering. Only I know how much this severe blow cost him. He partly dealt with it by writing a beautiful book, *Speaking with Bruno (Parlo con Bruno)*, in which he expressed all of a father's despair and the unshakable sadness that weighed on him from that moment on.

"In the evenings, when he would come home, I wouldn't dare ask him anything. Our maid Irma and I would arrange the newspapers next to his favorite armchair, hoping that he would manage to relax, even for a few minutes. At times our Persian cat, who would spend hours on your father's desk, would jump into this armchair. As your father arrived, Irma would wave it off the chair, but, with a tired gesture, he would indicate that the cat needn't be disturbed. Instead, he would take a few newspapers and sit on a stool."

CHAPTER 13

We Were Not Welcome in Switzerland

I've talked about the last time I saw my father on the morning of April 17, 1945, as he was leaving Villa Feltrinelli, headed for Milan. I later learned that while saying good-bye to my mother, he had said, "I'll be back in two or three days, at the most." She responded, "Come back as soon as you can. But please, let me know each day that you're alive."

We had to wait until April 23 before my father called for the first time. He said, "I'll be home tonight." An hour later, however, he called my mother again to let us know that he wouldn't be able to come. "Mantova has already been occupied and the Anglo-American troops have blocked the roads to Brescia. Even if I flew, I couldn't get by. Be patient and don't lose faith. Tell the children that we'll see each other very soon."

I was standing nearby as my mother and Il Duce spoke on the telephone. She interrupted him, almost screaming, "It's not true that the roads are blocked! They're deceiving you again! A little while ago a truck full of soldiers arrived here from Milan and they told me that they hadn't had any difficulties." I don't know what my father's exact response was. I only remember that I begged my mother to leave for Monza immediately and go to Villa Reale where he would be able to join us.

We arrived in Monza at dawn. At 8 A.M., my father called. He called again at 11 A.M. and then at 1 P.M. During this last call he told us that he had asked Gatti, his personal secretary, to take us to Como where we would have a country house at our disposal.

The house he was referring to was Villa Mantero, a large, gloomy building in which we would spend the fatal day of April 25th in complete isolation. According to what Il Duce told us, at the prefecture of Como we would be given two cans of gasoline—fuel was practically impossible to find—which would certainly have been enough for us to reach Switzerland and, if necessary, a destination even farther away.

We called the prefecture. An official answered, "We haven't received any orders here. And there's absolutely no gasoline." Then we called the archbishop of Milan, where Il Duce was meeting with Cardinal Schuster. They passed us to my brother Vittorio, who suggested we see his wife, who had been staying at Lake Como for some time, and ask her for gasoline.

On April 27, when we had already given up hope of hearing from him again and what would turn out to be the day before his death, my father called and asked to speak to me. He asked me to stay close to Mamma and I, in turn, asked him to be careful. I remember asking him, "Are you at least prepared to defend yourselves? Who is with you?" He responded, "There's no one left anymore, Romano. I am alone."

"But your personal guard," I insisted. "Your soldiers?"

And he said, "I don't know. They haven't arrived yet.

I don't even see my driver Cesarotti anymore. Even he must have left. Tell Mamma that she was right when she warned me not to trust him."

At this point, my mother took the receiver. In her memoir, she wrote, "Benito's voice was sad, and it stayed with me like a harrowing echo. It seemed impossible that everything should end like this, he facing his destiny alone and I unable to be near him. Romano and Anna Maria's pale and frightened faces brought me back to reality. There was nothing left for me to do but follow my husband's advice and take them to Switzerland before it was too late."

It was three in the morning when a black Lancia came to pick us up. We left Villa Mantero and I realized with disappointment that in the rush to pack my things in a single suitcase, I had left behind my lucky horn. I certainly never imagined that the Allied partisans who arrived in Villa Mantero the following day would later return it to me. At the time, however, not having the talisman with me seemed like a bad omen.

When we reached Ponte Chiasso on the Swiss border, I realized that many other cars had joined ours. In one of them, I recognized Buffarini Guidi, once one of my father's loyalists but later one of his betrayers, who had followed with the apparent hope of crossing the border with us.

My mother got out of the car and asked the border guards to let us through. One of them made a telephone call. Then, shaking his head, he said he had spoken with the Command Office in Bern and received orders to deny us entry. We later learned that there had been no communication between the guard and Bern. Evidently, the refusal was due to the guards' fears of running into problems by permitting Mussolini's wife and two of his children to enter Switzerland.

So we returned to Como. The Fascist Federation was in turmoil. Only after another hour's wait were we able to meet with a colonel we knew. He informed us that Il Duce had already left Como.

"And what about Pavolini's men, the three or four thousand he was waiting for?" I asked. The colonel responded that there had never been a Pavolini group and that my father had left for Valtellina so as not to lose any more time.

We also learned that my brother Bruno's widow, Gina, had spent several hours in the prefecture and that Il Duce had asked her several times whether the "small truck" had arrived. He was waiting for a van carrying a large quantity of highly classified documents that had been removed from a secret hiding place in the neighborhood of Gargnano on Lago di Garda.

Il Duce didn't know that on the afternoon of April 25, 1945, the documents he was waiting for were, in fact, loaded onto a small van. On board, in addition to the driver and an officer, was Maria Righini, a housekeeper from Romagna who had been in the service of my brother Bruno's family for many years.

Engine trouble caused the van to stop at Garbagnate where it had to be pushed into a farmstead courtyard. Maria walked for several kilometers before she was able to find transportation. She finally managed to reach Como, where she met Il Duce and told him what had happened. Three cars immediately left the prefecture heading for Garbagnate, but the town had already fallen into partisan hands. Nothing was ever heard about the van or its contents again.

My mother, sister, and I decided to leave the prefecture in Como and go to Valtellina. But this too proved impossible because the road to Dongo had already been blocked by Allied partisans. Fortunately, a soldier accompanied us to a small house on the outskirts of the city where one of his relatives had offered to help us. And so it was that while shots resounded throughout the city, Anna Maria and I slept, exhausted, in a small room in our unexpected sanctuary. We hadn't slept a wink for three nights.

When we awoke, the hunt for Fascists was in full swing. Peeking through the curtains, I saw a boy seized by the arms, held against a wall, and shot. The atrocious scene seemed more surreal because of the nature of the audience witnessing the execution—a group of disabled soldiers who had fled a nearby hospital, still in their pajamas.

I tried to convince my mother to turn herself, Anna Maria, and me in to the Liberation Committee set up in the prefecture. My mother, guided by her infallible intuition, realized that this would have been the wrong move. In the heat of the moment, we would have risked being placed against a wall and shot on the spot, solely because we bore the name *Mussolini*. Our host, who shared my mother's concern, consulted the police commissioner, who recommended that we not leave our shelter for any reason.

It was April 28 and our situation was truly dire. We

had no news of our father, or of my brother Vittorio, who had not been in touch with us since his telephone call advising us to go to Switzerland. "Only Edda," my mother said, "is safe right now. She's in a Swiss clinic with her three children."

My poor mother. From time to time, I would approach her and embrace her. Each time, I felt a tremor running through her body, with no signs of subsiding. Anna Maria sat on her bed, immersed in reading a history book. She didn't look up even when the echo of a series of explosions could be heard coming from outside.

I was convinced that the end was near. I approached the window and watched a bombing raid light up the sky above the city. I soon realized, however, that bombs didn't explode that way, and, strangely, the sky was being illuminated by something else. Only after I heard a voice from a loudspeaker yelling, "The war is over!" did I understand I wasn't witnessing a military operation but rather a celebration with fireworks.

Around 7 A.M. on April 29, American tanks entered the city. They were light vehicles, each with two soldiers facing the turret. Each soldier saluted the crowds by raising his right hand to his forehead. People left their houses cautiously at first, and then ever more enthusiastically and cheered. Around 11 A.M., we heard a radio communication broadcast via loudspeaker stating that many Fascist leaders had been killed by Allied partisans. Even Farinacci had been shot.

It was raining as if it were autumn. My mother and we children were waiting to hear and to understand more. We felt drained and incapable of any sort of reaction. As time passed, we became more convinced that death would be the only logical end to our long wait. My mother later told me, "When everything crumbles, when even the last hope vanishes, when the people who are dearest to us have left us, then thinking about the end becomes less onerous. These are the feelings that came into my mind on that April 29th, and I must confess that I would have wanted to be killed if not for the anguishing thought of leaving you and your sister alone."

It was almost noon when we heard slow and heavy steps approaching our room. The patron of the house came in holding a newspaper. He looked at us with an expression of mourning and placed the newspaper on a table.

Judging by the tears streaming down his face, he was convinced that we must have already known. Then I looked at the newspaper. It was a special edition of *L'Unità*. The entire front page was taken up by a single headline, in bold letters:

BENITO MUSSOLINI EXECUTED

The last act was thus completed.

AT THE END OF THE WAR, at least two high-ranking American officers were brought to justice for not preventing Il Duce's execution. I thought of this again with a somber clarity during the ceremonies taking place in Rome on June 4, 2004, in honor of American President George W. Bush. At least two of the American soldiers present in the capital during the president's visit, eighty-four-year-old Major Edward B. Thomas and eighty-year-old Sergeant Sam Finn, knew that General Eisenhower had ordered "Mussolini captured at all cost" and not placed before any unplanned proceedings ....

The American soldiers, especially those from the Black Devils Brigade that first entered Rome, were meticulously instructed on how to act toward Il Duce. They had already known for some time that he was no longer in the capital and that he had established a new Fascist Italian Republic in Northern Italy. They knew too that they wouldn't be the ones to capture him. Still, having just arrived in Rome, one of the first things they did was to go to Palazzo Venezia and enter the famous Sala del Mappamondo, which had been the seat of Il Duce's power for many years.

Sergeant Sam Finn was among those soldiers and said, "I was only twenty years old. I was happy, proud, excited. I went into Il Duce's empty office in Piazza Venezia together with my fellow soldiers from the Black Devils Brigade. I sat in Mussolini's chair and put my feet up on his desk. Then I went out and looked from the balcony. There was a mass of people yelling outside. I didn't speak Italian but I felt I had to say something to them. I raised my arms and yelled, "Viva l'Italia!"

Sergeant Finn's story made me think of the rare occasions when I too went into the famous Sala del Mappamondo. This is where my father was said to receive visitors without offering them a chair. It was on one of these occasions that I asked my father if this rumor was true. He explained, "Others in my position remove the chairs from their offices in order to gain a psychological advantage over their visitors. I, on the other hand, have them sit in front of me on the other side of the desk and look them straight in the eye. I assure you that when I want to, the effect I achieve is the same as if I had forced them to stay standing."

Il Duce used to enter Palazzo Venezia at 8:30 every morning except Mondays and Thursdays when he would first visit the king to confer with him and present him with documents for signature. I remember another rare occasion when members of my family were admitted to his office. It was 1938, I was eleven years old, and Papà wanted me to watch from the balcony a parade he had organized in honor of Hitler, who was visiting Rome for the second time in two years.

As Sergeant Finn would see years later, I saw a mass of people gathering on the square. If I didn't feel like screaming "Viva l'Italia," it was only because they were already doing so in a loud impressive chorus.

Those were the years of our greatest unity. Today it is difficult to understand what Fascism and the admiration of Il Duce meant for Italians.

.... Once I read the *L'Unità* headline, I didn't have the strength to touch the newspaper. I waited for my mother to come and read it. Anna Maria didn't move. She already understood and cried silently.

Everything was crumbling around us. The painful sensation I felt was that each of us was alone in the world. That afternoon (we hadn't left the room), a commissioner and two Allied partisans from the Liberation Committee came to arrest my mother.

She later told me, "I wasn't afraid, because without your father, my life no longer had any purpose. I was calm and already removed from everything. I only hoped that it would be over as soon as possible. When the commissioner ordered me to open the two suitcases I had brought from Gargnano, convinced that they would be full of documents and jewels, I almost wanted to laugh.

"He searched angrily, rummaging through my clothes until a small portrait of Bruno, which I never parted with, fell out of a small box. 'This belongs to the people,' he said, showing it to me. I felt compassion for him and for the ideas they had put inside his head. 'Of course it belongs to the people,' I replied. 'Because we Mussolinis always gave everything to the people. My son Bruno, the one in the portrait, even gave his life.'"

She was then taken to the police station for interrogation. We were permitted to follow her as far as the station. However, she was placed in San Donnino prison and we had no news of her until the following morning.

Even Anna Maria and I were arrested. The previous night, I had burned a series of valuable documents in a stove—these were all the letters and files that we had taken from Gargnano when we left Villa Feltrinelli for good.

What did those pieces of paper contain? Undoubtedly, there were several documents of historical significance. I remember some pertaining to the trial of Verona and others to my father's relations with Germany, France, and England, dated before the war began. They contained proof of Il Duce's efforts to prevent the conflict, an important subject whose relevance historians have only recently come to recognize.

There was also a file on the Savoia royal family, but not, as someone has suggested, a report on Prince Umberto's presumed "peculiar tendencies"—a report that I have never read and whose existence I personally doubt. No, the file I threw into the stove with the other documents was something much more important. It showed incontrovertibly that in the beginning, King Vittorio Emanuele III was not opposed to the war.

Today I regret having destroyed those documents, but I find absolution in the fact that I was eighteen years old at the time and was convinced, just as my mother and sister, that we only had a few hours to live. The radio continually announced that all of the Mussolinis would be indiscriminately shot. Put yourself in my shoes. Wasn't I perhaps right to think that if we were to be discovered in possession of Il Duce's documents, our identities would be immediately obvious and our chances of survival destroyed?

ON MAY 2, 1945, we were moved to Montecatini. Then the Americans handed us over to the English, who in turn transferred us to an internment camp in Terni.

After the sun went down and the watch-tower search lamps came on, beams of light would come into my shutterless room and I would think of my father's words, "Do you know what one of my weaknesses is, Romano? I cannot fall asleep if the shutters in my bedroom are not tightly closed."

I had the same weakness. And I would spend the long sleepless hours composing songs, before sleep would finally overcome me. All very sad, I have to say. The following days, I would perform these songs for Anna Maria on a secondhand accordion I had purchased with the little change we had left.

CHAPTER 14

My Mother's Dream

Our struggle to obtain my father's remains began immediately following his death in April 1945. Even before she was transferred to the English internment camp, along with Anna Maria and me, my mother had asked Gina, to see about having the body returned to us. Gina lived on Lago di Como and set to work on this task immediately. She quickly realized that accomplishing it would be difficult, but she couldn't have imagined just how difficult it would prove to be. In fact, not until twelve years later, on August 29, 1957, would the Italian government decide to return my father's body, which today lies in the San Cassiano cemetery.

News of the problems Gina was encountering reached us in Terni via a priest, who was also a relative. My mother was extremely disappointed, and once again, she learned what had happened through one of her extraordinary, illuminating dreams.

My father appeared to her unexpectedly on a narrow footpath strewn with holes and stones. His clothes were wet and torn, and his expression was troubled. My mother moved toward him and took him by the arms. He looked at her and appeared to brighten up, smiling

as he had so often done when he was alive and seen her
upset. My mother embraced him and, crying, asked if he
had suffered very much in his final moments.

"He told me not to worry," my mother recounts,
"because he hadn't felt any pain. Then he turned around
and I distinctly saw nine bullet holes in his back. He told
me that they were the work of a submachine gun but
that the bullets didn't hurt when they struck him. He
said, 'All you feel is a powerful heat and a bit of burning, but it's almost pleasing. Afterward, only a moment
later, you feel nothing.'"

At this point my mother awoke and rushed into my
room. When she opened the door, I was still awake. She
told me about her dream and wanted me to take her
back to her own bed where I spent the rest of the night
talking to her in a low voice.

Several days passed. Then, one of the nuns who
worked in the kitchen at which my mother was shortly
thereafter appointed manager, brought us a newspaper.
It ran an article on the autopsy conducted on my father's
body on April 30, 1945, by Professor Caio Mario
Cattabeni of the Institute for Legal Medicine in Milan.
The autopsy was performed "in order to reveal, aside
from the mortal wounds of the execution, the numerous
injuries caused by the angry mob, and, above all, any
possible illnesses from which Il Duce had suffered."

AT THIS POINT, allow me to digress. As noted, my
father's body was transported to Milan from Giulino di
Mezzegra on Lago di Como on the evening of April
28th, together with the bodies of Claretta Petacci and

the other Fascist leaders executed in Dongo. The vehicle containing the bodies arrived in Milan at 9:30 P.M. and stopped briefly at the Pirelli della Bicocca plant. An hour and a half later, the cadavers were deposited in front of a gasoline station in Piazzale Loreto, on the same spot where fifteen hostages had been executed on August 10, 1944. A Fascist pennant was placed in my father's right hand. His head was resting on Claretta Petacci's chest.

The rampage began at dawn on April 29 when a crowd began to vent its fury on the cadavers. Around 9 A.M., the bodies were hoisted upside down from the railing for all to see. They remained like this, on display, until that evening, when the American soldiers arrived. Not knowing whose bodies they were and believing them to be Allied partisans, the Americans honored them with a gun salute.

Professor Cattabeni's autopsy revealed that Il Duce's heart was "of a normal size with valves intact and no evidence of vulvular damage. Healthy myocardium. Coronary arteries unobstructed and healthy."

The aorta and the lungs were also in good condition, with no evidence of trauma despite the severe lesions produced by the beatings and the gun shots to the body. The spleen appeared to be "of normal size and appearance," as did the liver and the gall bladder, which were "unobstructed and healthy." And further, "Kidneys of a normal size. Renal glands healthy."

The autopsy concluded with an examination of the stomach, described as: "Large, with an even mucous membrane and the pylorus-duodenum mucous membrane intact, healthy. Nothing noteworthy in the small intestine and the colon, whose mucous lining appears to be completely normal."

There was a laceration on the large intestine, but the official autopsy specified that this was "a postmortem, posterior laceration caused by a projectile penetrating the right lumbar region."

At this point you may be wondering why illustrious doctors treated Il Duce for an ulcer for so many years when he hadn't suffered from any gastrointestinal problems. And there's another legitimate question to be asked. Who had for years been spreading and fueling the rumor that Il Duce had contracted syphilis as a young man and suffered from it throughout his life with devastating consequences on his mental capacity?

Both Professor Cattabeni's autopsy, performed on April 30, 1945, and Professor Antonio Cazzaniga's examination of the remains performed on August 14, 1946, found no trace of any scars or signs that a decades'-long ulcer or syphilis infection would have undoubtedly left. Therefore, there can be only one conclusion. In the latter case, these were rumors that were artfully spread as part of a stubborn and unrelenting campaign to disparage my father.

As for the fact that my father suffered from stomach pains in difficult moments, modern medicine explains how this sort of complaint often has psychosomatic origins that can be misleading because the symptoms are nearly identical to those associated with an underlying, identifiable medical cause. This explanation is even more compelling if we realize that doctors at that time did not have reliable diagnostic methods, which became available only after the war.

LET'S NOW RETURN TO MY MOTHER'S DREAM in which Il Duce appeared and said that he had been shot in the back with nine bullets from a submachine gun. The description in the newspaper corresponded exactly to what my father had revealed to my mother in her dream. Mamma then called Major Navarra, the commander of the Terni internment camp, and showed him the newspaper. Navarra was speechless. He already knew about my mother's dream and now here it was, in the papers, described in detail.

Meanwhile, my sister Anna Maria suffered greatly. Struck with polio at the age of nine, she required an anatomical corset for support but we had left it behind at Gargnano during the last days of the Salò Republic. Unable to obtain another one for her, we turned to the Red Cross for help, but all was in vain. We later learned that the one in Gargnano, whose value someone had estimated at 700 lira, had been confiscated and stored in a warehouse in Brescia.

And so our odyssey continued. On July 25, 1945, we were transferred from Terni to Forìo d'Ischia, where we remained for the duration of our confinement. My brother Bruno's widow, Gina, who learned where we were from the papers, wrote one day to tell us that her efforts to locate Il Duce's remains had been fruitless. She promised, nevertheless, to come and see us as soon as possible in order to tell the details of her search. She was

unable to keep her promise. A few days later, Gina trag-
ically lost her life by falling from a speedboat during a
storm on Lago di Como.

In April 1946, we again learned from the newspapers
that Il Duce's body had been stolen from plot number
348 in Musocco Cemetery in Milan. The whereabouts
of his body had, up to that moment, been kept in secret
even from us. Immediately thereafter, all traces of the
coffin containing the remains were lost. We later learned
that my father's body was kept until 1957 in Cerro
Maggiore Monastery before it was finally entrusted to
Father Carlo in Milan, the very same man who later
delivered it to my mother.

In the archives of Cerro Maggiore Monastery, there is
a document I was permitted to see. It reads, "The
remains of Mussolini were consigned to us on August
25, 1946, by the highly esteemed Father Mauro, who
had been sent by the Province Reverend Benigno da
Sant'Illario Milanese, in his turn approached by
Cardinal Schuster, Archbishop of Milan, in the name of
and on behalf of the Italian government. These remains
were stored in our monastery's interior chapel, on the
first floor, in a coffin placed to the side of the small altar,
and then, again, from 1950, in a cabinet reserved for
religious vestments, still in the same small chapel."

When she learned that Il Duce's body had been stolen
from the Musocco Cemetery, my mother turned to the
Italian minister for the constitution, Pietro Nenni, and
the chief constable of Milan, Vincenzo Agnesina, asking
that when the remains were recovered, they be returned
to us. She remembers, "Nenni behaved very humanely

and sent me a letter explaining that, unfortunately, for reasons of the State, he could not grant my request. I remembered then what Il Duce had written in his book *The Life of Arnaldo*, dedicated to his brother who died young: 'It would be enormously naive of me to ask to be left in peace after death. There can be no peace surrounding the tombs of those who lead these grand transformations we call revolutions.'"

When Alcide De Gasperi became president of Italy's Grand Council, we approached him too with a request for Il Duce's remains. One day, a carabiniere sent by the government appeared at Forìo d'Ischia and informed us that the request had been rejected. My mother then turned to Mario Scelba, who was later to become prime minister, but he responded rudely via a deputy of the Italian Social Movement. My mother suffered a great deal, yet she wouldn't give up, convinced that no government could deny her husband a Christian burial.

WHEN DE GASPERI DIED, he was succeeded by Giuseppe Pella who, as it turned out, would leave the position of council president only a few months later before we could even approach him with our request. It was the summer of 1953, and four long years were yet to pass before my father would find peace at San Cassiano.

The consigning of Il Duce's remains to my mother took place on August 29, 1957. Adone Zoli from Romagna was council president and Fernando Tambroni was minister of the interior. Giulio Andreotti, who would later become prime minister, had expressed a favorable opinion regarding the restitution of the remains, while Pietro Nenni, by then Italian minister for foreign affairs, declared he was "not opposed."

On the morning of August 28, my mother was first visited in Ischia by Paolo Baccanelli, a cousin of Council President Zoli. "Signora," he said, "you must leave at once, and alone. Not even your children may know where you are going." Later that morning she was also visited by Ischia's commissioner for public safety.

My mother left for Romagna in a black Lancia Appia, placed at her disposal by the prefect of Naples. Two plainclothes policemen, taking turns, drove her all the way to Villa Carpena in record time. "It was just after midnight," she later told me, "when we arrived at our destination. But I had to wait another twelve hours for the restitution."

At noon on August 29, in the small cemetery in San Cassiano, the chief constable of Milan Vincenzo Agnesina, Father Carlo of Milan, as well as the two professors who had performed the earlier autopsies, Cazzaniga and Cattabeni, handed my mother a wooden coffin containing Il Duce's remains. Professor Cazzaniga appeared particularly disturbed, and rightly so. In a glass container wrapped in newspaper, which he was holding under his arm, was my father's brain. It had been studied by neurologists in the laboratories of the Institute for Legal Medicine in Milan. A fragment had also been taken by the Americans, but it was not until March 25, 1966, that it was finally delivered to us by a government official from Washington. He came to Villa Carpena and informed us, "It was subjected to a criminology exam by specialists at the Walter Reed Institute near Washington. The results were negative."

I have often wondered how my mother found the strength to endure these terrible moments, especially the one at the cemetery in San Cassiano when the coffin was opened so that she could officially identify the body, as was required by chief constable Agnesina. I don't know how she could face such a test. Inside of her, I think, a defense mechanism was activated that helped her transform reality. If this hadn't occurred, her heart would not have held up.

"When they opened the coffin," my mother wrote, "everything seemed to disappear. I was only aware of a ray of light, which to me seemed like a ray of sunlight or a star, and then .... his face, Benito's face, when he was young and had a mustache, like in the photograph that hung by my bed after he died. With other loved ones I've lost, if I want to, I can imagine them as they were in the coffin. Him, no. Never. I was spared. How could I otherwise have continued to sleep, to eat, to function? Nature had mercy on me in that moment."

CHAPTER 15

A Few Words about Me

Up to this point, I have spoken about my father, about the years I spent with him, and about the numerous memories he has bequeathed to me. But I imagine that you may be curious to know a few more details about my subsequent personal life.

One of the undisputed joys of my life has been music.

After the war, in the house in Forli to which we were transferred, I was fortunate enough to find a grand piano. I had it tuned and began to play continually. I also continued playing the accordion. In 1947, thanks to the "Togliatti Amnesty," we were released as political prisoners and were once again free.

I was twenty years old, and a chance meeting influenced the rest of my life. It was a genuine stroke of luck. I met the famous guitar player Ugo Calise, and shortly thereafter formed a small jazz band with him and two other musicians. We played in small clubs. These were my first public performances, a baptism of sorts.

I remember the name of the club, La Conchiglia, where our quartet, the Jazz Star, made its first appearance by invitation of a friend. I played the accordion. It was a triumph! In Ischia, everyone welcomed us warmly and shared with us what little they had—grapes, milk, and tomatoes.

I later met Carletto Lombardo, who asked me to play with him. In 1949, we cut a record, *How High the Moon,* and it was then that my real career as a musician began. I also met internationally acclaimed artists such as Benny Goodman and Louis Armstrong, Duke Ellington and Oscar Peterson. At first, I feared that my last name would present an obstacle. Instead, I quickly realized that everyone was kind and pleasantly surprised to learn that Il Duce's son was a competent and able jazz musician.

I took up my interrupted school studies again, and, although I can't quite understand it, given my horrible relationship with mathematics, quickly earned an accounting degree in Naples. Upon my graduation, my mother wanted me to next enroll in the School of Economics and Business, so I did. But after taking several classes I developed a serious lung infection. The doctors said that the hardship suffered at the internment camp had had a damaging effect on my health. So I had to leave Ischia and settle down in Rocca di Papa, near Rome, where the mountain air was beneficial to my health. A short while later, my mother rented an apartment on Via Asmara in Rome in order to be near me. As soon as I completed my treatment with the famous lung specialist Professor Morelli, who was able to cure me completely within a year and a half, I moved to Rome as well.

How did I live in the years following the war? "My way," as Frank Sinatra said, or, to be more precise, doing a bit of everything and anything that came my way. In the 1950s, I raised chickens and pigs in Romagna. From time to time I would go to the open markets in Rome to sell them, and I confess that I've never earned as much since as I did during that time. With a friend, Diego Visco, who passed away in the mid-1990s, I also designed and sold advertising posters from a small open studio. I also hold dear what I've always considered to be my other occupation, second only to jazz, painting.

It was a certain clown named Burks I met while playing in a circus, who encouraged me to paint. "You're great," he would say. "This is the profession you were born for!" I don't think my mentor was right. Still, I have to say that over the years I've sold many paintings. With my earnings as a painter, I was able to fill the financial hole I had created when I got it into my head to become a movie producer and spend all the money I had on a terrible fiasco. In all, I have no regrets because I've learned a great deal from my mistakes, whether professional or personal.

The turning point in my life occurred in 1956 when I took part in the first jazz festival in Sanremo along with Nunzio Rotondo and Lilian Terry. When people found out who I was, there was an explosion of curiosity and attention surrounding me. I was accosted on the street for my autograph as if I were a movie star. Fans even found their way to wherever I was staying. In 1959, I met Sergio Bernardini, founder of the Bussola in Viareggio. He proposed that I play in a series of jazz concerts featuring the biggest names available. My name thus appeared on posters alongside jazz musicians who were already famous or destined to become so—among them were Gil Cuppini, Glauco Masetti, Franco Cerri, Lelio Luttazzi, Oscar Valdambrini, and Renato Sellani. Later, I played with Chet Baker, the legendary trumpet player, as well as with other big stars like Ella Fitzgerald and The Platters. I appeared on television for the first time with Fred Buscaglione right after Sergio Bernardini had signed him on together with Mina, Celentano, and Peppino di Capri.

For a half-century, jazz has been a source of tremendous satisfaction for me and it continues to be to this day. I have toured the United States, Asia, and Australia. At the beginning of 2004, I played in Moscow for the first time, with noted success. In Italy, I've traveled thousands of kilometers each year, holding concerts in big cities as well as in the country. I owe a great deal to some of the Italian musicians I've worked with, from Loffredo to Rotondo and Patruno.

I ADMIT THAT I HAVE ALWAYS BEEN A VAGABOND, even at the cost of being a terrible husband, or, at the least, a husband deserving of criticism. I have been married twice, the first time on March 3, 1962, to Maria Scicolone, with whom I have two daughters: Alessandra and Elisabetta. Alessandra went into politics early and achieved great success. She has made me a grandfather three times, and her youngest child, born in February 2003, is named after me. Just imagine my delight when I hold little Romano. The Italian law that children must take their father's surname has been relaxed for our family and we have been permitted to add his maternal name Mussolini to his paternal name Floriani.

Alessandra was nine years old and Elisabetta four when their mother and I separated. Another woman, Carla Puccini, had already entered my life and would later become my second wife. I met her in 1968 during a very painful time for me. My loving sister Anna Maria had died at the young age of thirty-nine, leaving behind two small children.

When I met Carla, she was performing with the Macario Theater Company in Torino. We have a daughter, Rachele, who was born in 1974. To be precise, Rachele was born in Wimbledon, England, because I was not divorced at the time and Italian law would not allow me to legally recognize her as my daughter.

Carla continued performing until 1980 when she left the stage. We were married in 1990. I am grateful to her for dedicating herself full-time to Rachele and me.